STANDARD
LOAN

UNLESS REC〜〜〜〜〜〜〜〜〜〜〜〜
THIS ITEM 〜〜〜〜 BE BORROWED FOR

FOUR WEEKS

To renew, telephone:
01243 816089 (Bishop Otter)
01243 816099 (Bognor Regis)

27. APR 01.

2 7 MAR 2010

- 2 MAR 2011

07. FEB 05.

13. FEB 06.

03. NOV 08.

The Development of School-Based Literacy

The Development of School-Based Literacy presents a model of social-contextual influences on children's literacy and literate language. Literate language is similar to the language teachers use and to the language used in reading books for young children. Based on a longitudinal study in homes and schools, Pellegrini and Galda present the results of how diverse and close social relationships influence children's literacy learning as they progress through the first three years of formal schooling, and discuss implications for teaching practice.

They suggest ways in which children can be taught to use literate language and to read and write. Being read to by parents at home is identified as particularly important, and different types of reading matter in the home are examined. In school, children's friends are important, and it is suggested that peers are helpful to the learning of literacy. Rather than separate friends as often happens in the classroom, Pellegrini and Galda suggest that interaction should be encouraged.

The Development of School-Based Literacy will be of interest to researchers and students of developmental and educational psychology, and to anyone interested in early cognitive and social development.

Anthony Pellegrini is a Professor of Educational Psychology and **Lee Galda** is a Professor of Children's Literature at the University of Minnesota.

International Library of Psychology
Editorial adviser,
Developmental psychology:
Peter K. Smith
Goldsmiths, University of London

The Development of School-Based Literacy

A social ecological perspective

Anthony Pellegrini
and Lee Galda

London and New York

First published 1998 by Routledge
11 New Fetter Lane, London EC4P 4EE

Simultaneously published in the USA and Canada
by Routledge
29 West 35th Street, New York, NY 10001

Typeset in Times by J&L Composition Ltd, Filey, North Yorkshire
Printed and bound in Great Britain by Biddles, Guildford and King's Lynn

British Library Cataloguing in Publication Data
A catalogue record for this book is available from the British Library

Library of Congress Cataloguing in Publication Data
Pellegrini, Anthony D.
    The development of school-based literacy : a social ecological
    perspective / Anthony Pellegrini and Lee Galda.
    p.   cm. – (International library of psychology)
    Includes bibliographical references and index.
    1. Language arts (Early childhood)   2. Literacy.   3. Reading
    (Early childhood)   4. Early childhood education–Parent
    participation.   I. Galda, Lee.   II. Title.   III. Series.
    LB1139.5.L35P45   1998
    372.6–dc21   98–14912
                                              CIP

ISBN 0–415–15393–X (hbk)

Contents

Chapter 1

Early literacy
Background and theory

A basic premise of this book is that becoming literate in the schools in most industrial societies involves learning a variety, or register, of what we have called 'literate' or 'school' language. While we believe that one register is inherently no better or worse than another for the purpose of communicating, learning the school language register seems to be an important precursor to becoming literate in schools. We argue that children's use of literate language is a very early form of school-based literacy.

In this chapter we will present our view of children's early literacy development by first discussing what it is we mean by 'developmental'.

A developmental view of literacy

Our orientation is a developmental one, involving a search for patterns and changes across the life span. It is a search for continuity and discontinuity across time, as well as across different situations, within the period of early childhood. To this end we discuss children's literacy learning from the preschool through the early primary grades, both at home and school. An important initial consideration is the way in which 'literacy' is defined. A developmental orientation suggests that literacy may be defined differently by individuals at different ages and in different contexts.

Our developmental orientation also includes consideration of the social ecological niche of literacy learning. Briefly, we consider the transactional relation between children and their environments, both in and out of school, as continuous or discontinuous between home and school interaction patterns and these patterns predict, respectively, school success or failure. We stress the ways in which social interaction between children and adults and children and peers structure children's social behavior and language.

It is important to stress our developmental orientation because it has important implications for the ways in which we define and measure literacy. Correspondingly, it also has implications for the ways in which literacy is taught in schools.

Qualitative and quantitative differences

Probably the most basic principle guiding our developmental orientation is that children are 'qualitatively' different from adolescents and adults. Such a notion is made clear in most stage theories of development that specify defining characteristics of children at different 'stages'. Qualitative differences, or differences in kind, are typically contrasted with quantitative differences, or differences in degree. Piaget (1983) provided some clear examples of these differences. For example, he suggested that the preoperational child sees the world in ways characterized as egocentric and nonconserving. Consequently, young children do not take others' points of view very well and cannot conserve basic identities. For preschoolers an array of candy canes arranged as follows: x x x x x would be considered greater than the following array: xxxxx. Thus, it is not simply a matter of seeing less of something; children see their world differently.

Further we view these qualitative differences as adaptive to the specific niche of childhood, not as imperfect variants of adult behavior. So, literate language is important for the period of childhood because it enables children to communicate with a variety of people from a variety of perspectives; it is not merely a step along the road to becoming literate.

Applied directly to literacy, quantitative differences in children's and adults' literacy status would be gauged in terms of degree. For example, children's literacy might be defined in terms of recognizing letters and a limited number of words. Adults, on the other hand, are able to read *more words*. In short, quantitative differences as applied to literacy would have children possessing *fewer* skills than adults. Pedagogical implications of this theory would have the adult model of literacy being broken down into its component parts. Children are then taught the individual components, from simple to more complex. Literacy is achieved when the individual parts sum to the adult model. This is not a developmental model in the sense that quantitative, not qualitative, differences separate children from adults.

In contrast, qualitative differences between children's and adults' literacy implies that child and adult literacy are different constructs altogether; they involve *different* skills. Children's skills are useful for their solutions to problems presented within childhood, as well as being useful for developing adult forms of literacy. Teaching children in this mode entails having them use literacy to solve their local problems, such as scribbling an imaginary grocery list or retelling a story. In short, qualitative differences are more basic and also allow a more positive focus on what children know and can do.

Continuity and discontinuity

It becomes a developmental task to chart the ways in which these qualitatively different constructs change across time. To undertake this task we must consider continuity and discontinuity in developmental processes. Continuity, as noted by Kagan (1971), can take two general forms: homotypic and heterotypic. Homotypic continuity involves similar responses across time. Kagan assumes that this sort of development is rare during the first ten years of life, a time when heterotypic continuity is more likely.

Heterotypic continuity, on the other hand, has the same underlying phenomenon expressing itself differently across time and it is very difficult to gauge. The ways that seemingly different phenomena at times 1 and 2 are interrelated are typically explained in terms of qualitative changes, or 'transformations', in structures. Such abrupt, and qualitative, changes are commonly observed in children around 2-years-of-age and again between 5- and 7-years-of-age. Thus the developmental antecedents of a 12-year-old's competence in one area, such as literacy, may have been expressed in a seemingly different area in kindergarten. Deciphering this level of 'cryptography' (Kagan, 1971: 15) is a daunting task. We assume, in these cases, that children are changing rapidly and we also assume that there is underlying stability. The obvious question is how do we know what to look for in gauging heterotypic continuity?

Guidance in developmental inquiry should, of course, come from theory. Theory tells us what is important and why it is important. Further, it also (should) tell us where to look to uncover hidden continuities. Where theory does not provide explicit guidance in the search for continuity researchers (from a variety of disciplines) rely on 'design feature arguments'. By design features we mean structural and physical aspects of behavior that are similar across time. We assume that the earlier behaviors are functionally related to later behaviors. An example of a structural design feature would be alternating roles.

Many forms of young children's play are characterized by reciprocal roles, such as alternating between chaser and chased in vigorous play. Continuity in design features can be observed in the games of older children (players alternate between offense and defense modes). In the specific case of literacy development, design features of children's oral language, especially the sorts of language used when children are being read to and when they are engaged in social pretend play, are similar to the features of school-based literacy. However, similarity between sets of design features does not guarantee that they are functionally related. The antecedent may lead to a consequence that does not resemble it. Similarly, consequences could have origins in antecedents with which they do not share design features.

It may be the case, for example, that there is little continuity across development and the behaviors utilized in childhood are unique to that period, and then become irrelevant in adulthood. Our position is that literate language is both important to the niche of childhood and important to subsequent development.

In the next section we discuss different definitions of literacy and their often implied rather than explicitly stated theories of learning or development.

Individual differences

Another basic tenet of a developmental orientation is that, despite regularities in development as indicated in stage-like progression, individual differences exist. Individuals and their environments influence each other in a dialectical fashion. Not all children proceed through the developmental process in the same way or at the same rate. By extension, not all children become literate in the same way. The systems theory notion of equifinality posits that there is more than one route to competence. Equifinality reminds us again that the relations between antecedents and consequences are very complex.

Our conceptualization of development also recognizes the unique contributions that individuals make to the developmental process. Individual differences, often expressed in terms of children's temperament, mediate the transaction between children and their social environments. We must take account of individuals' con- we consider development something more than a uni- cultural reproduction process (Tooby and Cosmides, 1992).

Cultural reproduction models of development are unidirectional to the extent that the values and practices of society are directed at and internalized by children with little consideration for the ways in which individuals (independent of society) affect their environments.

Temperament and relationships

Temperament is an excellent construct to gauge individuals' contributions to the developmental process in that it has a biological expression, appears very early in life, and is stable across the life span. Children with a certain temperament, for example, sociable, extroverted children, may seek out a variety of different social partners with whom to interact. These children might come to learn literate language by interacting with a variety of others and taking on a variety of roles. By interacting with others from a variety of backgrounds children learn to explicate the meaning of their messages so that they can be understood by those with whom they may share minimal background.

Children who are less social and introverted may interact with fewer social actors than their more social counterparts. Their social relationships may be characterized as intensive or 'close relationships', such as friendships. Children may learn literate language in this sort of relationship through the conceptual conflicts and resolutions that typify close relationships (Hartup, 1996). That is, friends, compared to acquaintances, are more likely to disagree with each other. These disagreements, because they are important to the participants, are closely monitored, remembered (Dunn and Slomkowski, 1992), and usually resolved in the interest of maintaining the relationship. By monitoring conceptual conflict and working toward resolution children become aware of their friends' feelings and needs. They, in turn, monitor their own behavior so as to accommodate to those needs. This sort of perspective taking is an important psychological precursor to affective communication, both oral and written (Jones and Pellegrini, 1996; Pellegrini *et al.*, 1984b).

Of course individual differences are mediated by larger societal mores. It may be the case, for example, that children are discouraged from taking a variety of roles. As we will discuss below, 'positional' socialization orientations limit children's role experiences: children are restricted to certain roles, due to their being a 'child' or a 'girl'.

Dialectical relationships

The final aspect of development that we will discuss is the dialectical relation between individuals and their environments. Socialization theories of development posit a unidirectional force from society to the children. As we noted in our discussion of individual differences, we consider development a dialectical, or transactional, process. Children influence their environments and their environments influence them. Some of the best examples of this transactional relation come from child language (Ninio and Bruner, 1978; Pellegrini *et al.*, 1995b) and the mother–child interaction literature (Snow, 1972). In cases where mothers read and talk to their children they gauge the sophistication of their interaction strategies and talk to children's levels of sophistication. When we consider the twin notions of child effects on the environment in conjunction with individual differences a clearer picture of the transactional nature of development emerges. Individual children self-select themselves into environments which are supportive of their temperament; for example, choosing a certain peer group. In this way they affect their environment. The environment, which might be composed of certain children, in turn affects the child by providing models for social behavior.

Development involves children changing across time. The nature of the change, we think, is qualitative in the sense that children at different periods of life see the world differently. Individual development is embedded in an ecological matrix where children and their social and physical environments affect each other. We now consider in detail the ways in which literacy develops and the ways in which individual children learn literacy at home and at school.

What is literacy?

Literacy, as Wolf and colleagues (1988) at Harvard Project Zero note, can be defined very broadly, in terms of creating and interpreting various symbol systems, such as maps, music scores, graphs and traditional alphabetic scripts. In this book we are concerned not only with literacy in alphabetic scripts but also with the specific form of alphabetic script used in schools. At the simplest level, literacy in this context means being able to read and write school-based texts. Part of this process invariably involves children being able to use the sort of oral language which characterizes literacy instruction. Moving beyond this simple level, we must ask ourselves what exactly we mean by reading and writing. We suggest that the nature of literacy varies in functional terms, as well as according to the developmental status of the learner.

By functional we mean that literacy has many different uses, and consequently is defined differently, in different communities. So reading (in the form of singing) from a hymnal is one form of literacy that differs from reading required on a standardized test or in a children's book at school. Similarly for writing, the variety of writing required to convey a telephone message to a friend is very different from that required in a school essay. Scribner and Cole's (1978) categorization scheme for literacy among the Vai captures this functional variety quite nicely. One level of literacy is not learned in school and is used for personal needs. Examples of this include writing to complete an application, to make a grocery list, or used as a mnemonic aid. Another form of literacy is that which is used in religious ceremonies, such as Koranic literacy or Scripture reading. This sort of literacy is learned across a long period of time in formal settings but is different from school literacy, or the type of literacy taught in western schools. School-based literacy is also taught across a long period of time but it entails reading and writing about specified topics.

Being literate in one area often does not include similar levels of facility in another area. Applying these findings to children in western schools, we have instances, as we will illustrate in later chapters, where children and mothers are literate in one area (a personal, non-schooled type of literacy) but they are not very facile with school-based texts. The design features, or rules for interacting with the print and the participants of the two events, in these two literate events are dissimilar.

School-based literacy is something that must be taught either implicitly or explicitly. It is not 'acquired' in the same sense that oral language is acquired. Virtually all individuals (under conditions ranging from highly supportive to highly restrictive) develop aspects of oral language that render them functional, while many individuals do not become literate. Further, no scholars, to our knowledge, have suggested a biological program for literacy as they have for oral language development (e.g. the Language Acquisition Device). Where literacy seems to be learned 'naturally', as in cases of precocious readers described by Durkin (1966) and Clark (1976), the home environment in which literacy is learned is very close to the environment of school. For example, these children are read to frequently by parents, the books that are read are similar to those used in school literacy events, and the sort of talk that surrounds home literacy events is similar to the talk of school literacy events (Bernstein, 1960, 1972; Cook-Gumperz, 1973; Heath, 1983; Scollon and Scollon, 1981). In this case, the design features of school and home literacy are isomorphic.

Thus, school-based literacy is only one very specific variety of literacy, much like an oral language register. It is no better or worse than other types of literacy; it just happens to be used in a certain social situation. However, access to this register is necessary for success in school, and probably in society at large.

The specific case of school-based literacy

While there are different varieties of literacy, when we speak of literacy we typically mean school-based literacy. Even when 'functional' definitions of literacy are proffered, such as UNESCO's (Harman, 1970), school grade level criteria are stipulated: 'A person is literate who can, with understanding, read and write a short, simple statement on his [sic] everyday life' (Harman, 1970: 226). This functional definition is often coupled to a grade completion criterion of fourth or fifth grade.

Psychometric definitions

An all too simple definition of literacy in school is in terms of some performance outcome on a measure, such as a norm-referenced 'grade equivalent score' or a criterion-referenced list of skills. While some tests can and indeed do measure early school-based literacy we suggest that defining literacy in terms of these scores on these measures is limited. It is limited, we think, because it confuses the directionality in defining a psychological construct such as literacy with the process used to measure it. Psychological constructs should be defined theoretically before they are defined, and measured, psychometrically. Psychometric definitions used to define literacy reverse this logic: it takes test scores or other discrete skills which are indicative of literacy and uses them to define the construct, literacy. Thus literacy becomes defined as the ability to recognize letters and produce their corresponding sounds. While phoneme–grapheme recognition is an important component in learning to read and write, it is only one small correlated dimension of the larger social cognitive process of learning literacy. This larger process is what needs defining. Then we can develop measures to assess it.

Decontextualized language

The type of literacy taught in schools has often been described as 'decontextualized' in the sense that meaning is conveyed primarily through linguistic means, with minimal reliance on contextual cues and shared assumptions. If a speaker, for example, wanted to identify a car in the car park, literate language would encode critical information about the car (make, year, color) as well as the location (lot A, aisle 5, in the middle). More contextualized language might rely on shared knowledge (e.g. It's near the place we used to park) or context (e.g. pointing to the location).

Literacy also entails the fictionalization of the 'self' (Scollon and Scollon, 1981). This involves treating oneself, as well as others, as generalized others, with whom one shares little knowledge. The communicative implication of this stance is that meaning must be 'lexicalized', or explicitly encoded in language. The ability to distance from and reflect upon one's audience is crucial to literacy (Applebee, 1978). The literate communicator conveys meaning so that this generalized other can comprehend the message. Because of the generalized, and distant, nature of one's audience, communicative strategies which rely on shared knowledge assumptions and gestures do not effectively communicate meaning.

Literate events in school, or those events where individuals interact around print, are typically characterized by 'literate language'. The language of the books that children read and the language that children produce, both in writing and while talking with teachers and peers, during literacy events, is also 'literate'. Take the example of children reading books. In texts for young children, pictures are the supportive context which help children decode meaning expressed in the lexicon. As children progress through school, this supportive context is increasingly minimized as meaning must be inferred from the text primarily. Similarly, when talking to the teacher about a story with which both teacher and child are familiar, the child should assume the teacher is naive, and explicitly encode meaning.

These two aspects of the social context of school literacy (decontexualized and assuming a fictionalized self) have an effect on the structure of language that occurs there. Some linguists, particularly those associated with the Prague Circle (e.g. Fribas, 1966; Halliday, 1967; Vachek, 1964), argue that the structure of language is determined by its function. Halliday's theory, as expressed in his work on transitivity and theme (Halliday, 1967) and cohesion (Halliday and Hasan, 1976), represents one very systematic exposition of this 'functional sentence perspective' in linguistics.

In Halliday's model, decontextualization determines the structure of 'literate language'. At the word level, fictionalized others are encoded in third person pronouns and individual words which reflect a common theme (e.g. lexical cohesion). At the sentence level, syntactic structure (subject/predicate) reflects the information structure of the message. Background, or given information, is encoded in the syntactic subject and new information is encoded in the predicate. At the text level, meaning in one sentence is tied to other sentences (e.g. The *car* is black. *It* is in row A).

Metalanguage

As children learn to use language for different purposes and in different situations, they reflect upon the language system *per se*. In order to produce and comprehend the sorts of language that minimally rely on context and maximally rely on linguistic features, children must choose from a variety of linguistic options to realize their meaningful intentions. Thus, decontextualization and fictionalized self features of literate language should have the correlated benefit of stimulating children's metalinguistic awareness, or awareness of the rules and options governing language and its use in social context. Children's awareness of language and literacy can be inferred from their use of terms about language, e.g. **talk**, **say** and **listen**, and literacy events, e.g. **book**, **pencil** and **read** (Pellegrini *et al.*, 1995a).

Narrative

There is another design feature which is particularly important in primary school children's literacy events and that is the rhetorical genre of the typical literacy event: narrative. Children in the early years of school are exposed frequently to texts written in the narrative, or story, mode. Stories, like literate language, have fictionalized characters, are characterized by richly descriptive language, and are temporally and causally motivated. In short, the stories that children are read and write should have cohesion and elaborated noun phrases, and various types of conjunctions to conjoin phrases (Pellegrini *et al.*, 1984a).

The design features of school-based literacy and the ways in which they are realized linguistically are displayed in Figure 1.1.

Design features	Linguistic realization
Decontextualization	New/old syntax
	Cohesion
	Adjectives
Fictionalized self	Third person pronouns
	Cohesion
Metalanguage	Language about language and literacy
Narrative structure	Varied use of conjunctions
	Adjectives

Figure 1.1   Design features of school-based literacy

Literacy learning: developmental and social ecological considerations

A developmental orientation to literacy learning suggests that the oral language skills children are learning in different 'literate events' at home and in their larger community relate to school-based literacy. We suggest that the similarity in design features between certain home and school literacy events provides guidance to charting developmental continuity. Following the work of sociologists, such as Bernstein (1960, 1982), anthropologists, such as Scollon and Scollon (1981) and Heath (1983), and educators, such as Clay (1977), Olson (1977) and Snow (1983), we believe that the critical design features for school-based literacy involve decontextualization, fictionalization of self, use of metalanguage, and narrative competence. The developmental task involves locating the speech events in children's experiences before they enter school that support their use of literate language.

Variety of social roles and design features

Our social ecological orientation guides us to examine the locations in which and processes by which children learn to use literate language. This involves a search of home and community speech events which share design features with literate language. Social scientists, most notably Bernstein (1960, 1982) and his students (e.g. Cook-Gumperz, 1973), and anthropologists, such as Gumperz (1986), Heath (1983) and Schieffelin and Cochran-Smith (1984), have examined the socialization of what we have called literate language. There is striking similarity across these discussions of language, school and literacy to the extent that they all define school-based literacy as a linguistic register indigenous to mainstream culture.

These scholars argue that literate language and school-based literacy are extensions of the ways in which children are socialized to interact with each other and adults and the ways in which they convey meaning. The rules of these 'speech events' (Hymes, 1967) are learned by children so that they know how to act and speak in specified situations. Thus, competence in language use is not determined in terms of some abstract and implicit knowledge of syntactic rules, but instead in terms of role-appropriate, communicative competence (Bernstein, 1972; Hymes, 1967). Communicative competence involves knowledge of the socially accepted options for social behavior and language in a variety of situations. These situations, or speech events, are rule governed in terms of social and linguistic norms. Similarity in design features exist between speech events, generally, and literacy events specifically, in most middle class homes and schools. Similarity exists between home and school for the social roles that children take and the forms of language that children use.

Social roles

One of the most thorough and perhaps one of the most controversial explanations for the socialization of literate language comes from Bernstein (1960, 1971, 1972, 1982). He suggests that conveyance of meaning is determined by one's role-assignment and flexibility in the socialization context. He specifies four socialization contexts: the regulative context (where children are made aware of the moral order and rules), the instructional context (where children learn skills and about objects and people), the imaginative context (where children are encouraged to experiment and re-create the world in their own terms), and the interpersonal context (where children become aware of their own and others' affective states). Children in different groups are socialized to take different roles in these contexts.

These different socialization practices have direct implications for children's language use. Take the regulative context. If children are treated according to a 'positional' orientation, their language and social experiences are limited to culturally determined roles; for example, children must always obey parents, without question. Parents set out guidelines without providing rationales or expecting feedback from children. The implication of this orientation is that children do not have to verbally explicate meaning in order to be understood: meaning can be conveyed by virtue of one's assigned social role. Such limited role experiences (they are only recipients of orders) and the language used in these situations may evidence a paucity of appeals based on reasoning and causal conjunctions (e.g. Do this *because* it's your turn). These sorts of socialization contexts are typified by strictly defined power relationships. Parents, by definition of their roles, give orders and children, correspondingly, comply without question; this is exemplary of Bernstein's notion of strong classification (Bernstein, 1982).

By contrast, a person-centered orientation involves looser power relationships. Roles are more likely to be based on reasoning, not assigned position. Consequently in a regulative context children must define their social role by appropriate social and linguistic behavior; they cannot merely step into a positionally defined role. Part of the process of defining role, according to Bernstein (1972), entails making role relationships opaque. Children in these circumstances reflect upon their roles and those of the interlocutors and follow role appropriate social and linguistic rules. In short, the person-centered orientation socializes children to a 'fictionalized self' orientation, to verbally explicate meaning, and to reflect upon the rules of different speech events.

When children from positional- and person-oriented traditions go to school they often encounter an institution that does not encourage (or indeed tolerate) deviations from accepted social behaviors and registers; this is Bernstein's (1982) notion of a strong frame. Thus, children who have learned the language of school are speaking the socially accepted register of school; other language varieties are not tolerated. The implications for school success then become painfully clear and predictable. That these socially accepted registers can be learned in school is a powerful dimension of Bernstein's theory. Bernstein's theory is clear, unlike more fatalistic theories (e.g. Gee, 1989), which put forth a variant of the 'critical period hypothesis' (i.e. if you haven't been socialized to learn school language by the time you enter school, it is nearly impossible to learn it). In his theory, children can learn the school register by weakening the frame and classification systems in schools, and other socialization contexts (e.g. churches, youth groups).

Socialization styles

Earlier we noted that Bernstein's theory was controversial. Much of the controversy related to discussions of class differences and socialization contexts. Bernstein's theory stimulated a massive amount of research in the UK (e.g. Tizard and Hughes, 1984; Wells, 1984) and in the USA (Hess and Shipman, 1965) and in many cases the hypothesized class differences (in the UK) and the hypothesized class and race differences (in the USA) were not supported. A more basic dimension of the theory has been supported, however. That dimension relates to the way in which children's socialization contexts affect social behavior, language and school success. Research in this area does support Bernstein's basic notion of role assignment and flexibility.

Drawing from the literature on family socialization, a consistent picture emerges. Children reared in homes characterized as 'authoritative' (Baumrind, 1989) are more socially competent (this includes school-based achievement) than children in other socialization arrangements. Authoritative parenting practices are generally defined as responsive to children's needs, yet demanding. Steinberg and colleagues (1992) have further illustrated that autonomy granting and democratic orientations within an authoritative style are particularly important in predicting school success. Examples of democratic and autonomy granting orientations include parent–child joint decision making. This orientation is strikingly similar to Bernstein's person-oriented socialization style. Also like Bernstein, Steinberg and colleagues suggest that children can learn these orientations at home or in their peer groups; thus they are not 'trapped' by their home context. In short, we recognize that school-based literacy is culturally bound and that middle class children, more frequently than working class children, succeed, at least partially, because of the cultural continuity between home and school. We also recognize that children can succeed in school if they are given multiple and varied opportunities to shape their own future.

Relationships and literate language

In the preceding section, we suggested that the flexibility and variety of roles which children took facilitated children's learning literate language. Relationships, following Hinde (1978), are interactions between individuals across time. Thus, Jack and Sam have a history of interactions and a special relationship; they are friends. Jack's interactions with Sam will differ from his interactions with Joe, who is an acquaintance, not a friend. Knowing about relationships helps us understand and predict the nature of individuals' interactions in different social arrangements. Close relationships, such as friendships and sibling relationships and attachment relationships (or the relationships between a mother and her child), are characterized by an emotional component that distinguishes them from other social arrangements.

Close relationships of the sort noted above are typified by an emotional component indicative of trust and investment. When friends of a securely attached child and his or her mother interact together, they trust each other and they enjoy each other's company. This emotional component may be particularly important for children learning literate language to the extent that these relations afford opportunities to reflect upon social interactive process and corresponding language forms. The ability to reflect upon language and social processes is an important component in literacy development. Specifically, friends, compared to non-friends, tend to disagree and then compromise frequently (Hartup, 1992). Further, children in close relationships tend to monitor and remember the details of their interactions (Dunn, 1988; Dunn and Slomkowski, 1992). Evidence of children's monitoring of the social interactive processes includes children's talk about 'internal states', such as emotions and language. Indeed, this monitoring, and the corresponding concern with maintaining the interaction, is probably an important component in children's willingness to compromise.

While we have argued that close peer relationships and their corresponding forms of reciprocal interaction foster 'meta' processes, it is also the case that close adult–child relationships and their complementary interaction styles also afford children with opportunities to reflect upon the social interactive process. We know from the attachment literature, for example (Bus and vanIJzendoorn, 1988, 1995), that interaction between securely attached children and their mothers is coordinated and mothers adjust their styles so as to maximize children's participation in the interaction process. This process of children 'appropriating' task responsibility is an important precursor of metacognitive processing in Vygotskian theory (see Wertsch, 1979 for an extended discussion of Vygotsky's theory). For example, when mothers talk with children in storybook reading contexts they often ask children to plan (What comes first?) and to evaluate information (e.g. Did he really say that do you think?). Mothers also model cognitive and linguistic terms which children then use later (Pellegrini *et al.*, 1995b). In short, children learn to 'go meta' on the literacy events through interactions in close relationships. In close peer relationships, conflicts and resolutions seem to facilitate reflection. In close adult–child relationships, mothers' ability to engage children in literacy events may effect reflective processes.

Conclusion

In this chapter we have discussed school-based literacy from a developmental, social and ecological perspective. We defined school-based literacy in terms of facility with language characterized by 'meta' talk, fictionalized self, decontexualized language, often embedded in narratives; this constitutes literate language. We posit that children's socialization histories, both in the home and with their peer group, have important implications for the social role and rules they learn. These socialization experiences, in turn, affect children's learning of literate language. Following Bernstein's theory we would expect that children socialized to take on different roles and interact with a variety of people would develop literate language as a consequence of these varied social experiences. It may also be the case that the quality of the social relationships are important, rather than just diverse experiences. In close peer and adult relations children learn to monitor the interactive process such that they treat the rules of literacy as opaque and consequently are capable of 'going meta' on these rules. This 'meta' ability is crucial in school-based literacy learning. The following chapters explore these ideas through a series of research projects designed to explore literacy at home and at school.

Chapter 2

Methods in the study of children's literacy development at home and at school

In Chapter 1 we argued that children's literacy develops out of the variants of oral language used in various social roles and relationships at home. The continuity between the design features of home and school literacy events is crucial for success in school literacy learning. Consequently, we must consider data collection procedures both at home and at school. In this chapter we situate the discussion of the specific data collection procedures used in our work in a larger historical frame. Consideration is given to the various ways in which other scholars have studied children's literacy development at home and at school and how these methods influenced our own methodological choices. Generally and within each of these settings, we both consider naturalistic and contrived designs.

Methodological considerations in the study of early literacy development

By naturalistic we mean studying children in their everyday circumstances. Contrived settings, on the other hand, are analogues of these naturalistic settings. Analogue situations can utilize experimental designs to control extraneous variables and manipulate theoretically relevant variables in the service of causal explanations. Analogue situations can also involve the use of psychometric testing procedures where hypothetical situations are presented to the child or the adult and their responses are recorded.

Within either naturalistic or analogue research orientations, data collection procedures can be direct or indirect. By direct we mean that the data are derived from the participants' actual behaviors and language. Direct observations of children's language at home might have an observer recording a child's language as it occurred. An indirect method of collecting child language data might involve mothers answering questions about or recording, *post hoc*, examples of children's oral language production. A matrix illustrating dimensions of data collection orientations, and corresponding examples, is presented in Figure 2.1.

Children at home

Studying children at home is difficult but also very important given the influence of home and community on children's school performance. The many roles into which children are socialized at home and in their communities have enormous impact on their school performance. Certainly, literacy events at home impact children's literacy learning at school. Thus no matter how difficult to obtain, home data are essential to understanding children in school.

Naturalistic methods: direct

The difficulty of *direct* home observations is related in large part to logistics and reactivity. Logistically, conducting home observations involves a multi-step process.

Scheduling

It is crucial that both researchers and participants have reliable means of communication. At a minimum it is necessary for each party to have a telephone in service. Telephones are necessary for scheduling home visits, notifying a party if an observation has to be canceled, and confirming an upcoming home visit.

	Home		School	
	Direct	Indirect	Direct	Indirect
Natural				
	Observing	Mother's diary	Observing	Teacher's diary
Analogue				
	Experimental	Parents responding	Experimental	Diary
	Hypothetical	to lessons	Teacher checklist	Checklists
		situations		
		Diary		

Figure 2.1 Data collection orientations

Participants and researchers must schedule a time that is mutually agreeable. The choice of time is often a compromise between the time that is theoretically relevant for the research question and convenience. For example, observing mothers reading to children at bed time may not be possible because parents may not want a researcher in their homes at bed time. Procedures for timely notification of cancellation of home visitation appointments should also be explicated. When appointments are set, we have found it helpful to call the home the night before the observation to confirm the time.

In our home observation projects issues of safety complicated the process. Observers rightfully felt uneasy about visiting strange neighborhoods, often at night, alone. This necessitated using two researchers per visit.

Organization and set-up

Once appointments are made the researchers must then load equipment and proceed to the site. To minimize the problem of forgetting crucial materials and equipment we kept 'kits' for our home visits. The kits included: address and phone number of the home, a map of the area, a flash light (to spot house numbers), research props, video camera, audio recorder and extra tapes and batteries.

Upon arrival, the process of setting up begins. It is important to observe the phenomenon of interest under normal conditions. For example, if the mother usually reads to children in their bedroom, the observer should be set up there.

Reactivity

Of course, having an observer present is hardly 'normal'. While we recognize that the effects of observers' presence in the situation being observed never really disappear, we can minimize these effects. In order for participants to habituate to the researchers' presence, the researchers need to spend a substantial period in the home, before the actual data collection process begins. It is also helpful to have a member of the community being studied included in the research team. In our work, initial home visits served this purpose. In some of our work we also had an adult with whom the caregiver was familiar in the home with us. In this visit the researcher 'visited' with the mother, talking about the child's interests and being shown around the house. After this informal beginning, caregivers were interviewed by the researchers using procedures specified in the HOME Inventory (Caldwell and Bradley, 1984).

More habituation time is usually needed when the data collection procedures are unusually obtrusive. For example, using a video camera in the home requires a longer habituation period than when using a checklist. Indeed some researchers (e.g. Dunn, 1988) do not use video cameras at all because they are considered too obtrusive. Where videotaping is crucial to the research question, it makes sense to introduce it after the initial habituation period, allowing for another period of habituation to the equipment. It may also be necessary to explain and demonstrate to children how the equipment works and allow them to look through the camera and to view the recordings made.

Timing the observations

The duration of the observation is also important to consider. Longer and repeated observations of target events usually maximize the possibility of collecting representative data. In cases of event or behavior sampling observations of a specific event are desired; the duration of the observation is defined by the length of the event itself. In other cases, we may sample a time period and make observations within that period, recording behavior as it naturally occurs. The durations here vary according to logistical and theoretical constraints. Choice of a sampling duration does, however, impact on the sorts of data available. For example, Haight and Miller (1993) found that only after the first hour of an observation did they observe mothers and children (at 36- and 48-months) engaging in sophisticated forms of play. In their longitudinal study of mother–child play in the home children were observed at 12-, 24-, 36- and 48-months of age within individual observational period durations ranging from 1.6 to 4.2 hours.

If observers do not have long periods to spend in the home, waiting for the event to occur, it might be useful to find out in advance the approximate time the target event usually occurs. Researchers might ask the caregivers in advance for the time and show up before that time. Alternately, and as will be discussed below, times for specific literacy events might be derived from diaries kept by caregivers.

Taped data

Obviously direct observations are expensive, obtrusive and in some cases impossible to implement. There is one method which utilizes a form of direct observations in the home but minimizes many of the logistical and reactivity problems. This process involves the use of remote audio recorders. Two sorts of tape recorders can be used: simple cassette recorders or voice-activated recorders. Starting with the simpler method of using a cassette recorder, the researcher provides each family with a tape recorder, a supply of cassettes and batteries, and a schedule for turning on and shutting off the recorders. Observers also tell families where to place the recorders; for example, at the dinner table during the evening meal (e.g. DeTemple and Beals, 1991). Tapes are collected at the end of specified periods.

With voice-activated tape recorders, machines are left in a target location and begin recording with the onset of language and stop when the language ends. The benefits of these methods are readily apparent: large amounts of data can be collected simultaneously with relatively low costs. Persistent problems with this method include maintaining schedule/sampling fidelity and the frequency of malfunctioning machines.

Naturalistic methods: indirect

Given these difficulties with direct, naturalistic observations in the home, it is not surprising that researchers have explored the use of indirect techniques (Pellegrini, 1996). By indirect we mean collecting naturalistic information without actually being at the research site.

Remote sampling

One interesting possibility is the use of 'remote sampling' (Bloch, 1989; Pellegrini and Stanic, 1993) whereby participants are contacted at predetermined intervals and asked to respond to a series of standardized questions. An example of such a standardized form is presented in Figure 2.2.

While remote sampling has great promise for gathering information in hard to reach areas, it is limited by availability of telephones and children's presence in the home at the time of the call. Children may be playing in another room, outdoors, or at another location, thus not directly observable.

Social desirability is also problematic with these sorts of formats. Interviewees may give the sorts of information they think the interviewer wants to hear (e.g. John's reading a book in his room) rather than more accurate information (e.g. John's playing Nintendo).

Focal Child _____ Caller _____ Date _____ Time _____

Call: Original   Callback I   Callback 2

QUESTIONS
Where is (X)(the focal child)? _____

Can you see him/her?   Yes   No
Who is he/she with?

	Name	Age	Relationship
I			
2			
3			
4			
5			

What are they doing?

Are they using paper, pencils, or books?   Yes   No

How?

Figure 2.2 Remote sampling form

Diary methods

Diary methods are another, time-honored, approach to conducting indirect observation in natural settings. They were used by Charles Darwin (1977) in studies of his son, and have been a mainstay in the child language literature. Diary studies involve providing caretakers with varying degrees of structure, and asking them to make entries at various points.

Researchers can provide varying degrees of structure on the diary formats. The degree of structure provided is directly related to the standardized levels of the data derived from the diary. With a low structure format care providers note behavior that they consider important at times that suit them. It may be that recordings are made very soon after the memorable event in the first stages of the diary project. Then as the novelty of the project declines, recordings are made after a longer duration, with less frequency, and with less detail.

By introducing some structure we can help make the records more systematic across a long period of time. For example, behavior can be systematically sampled by asking that entries be made on a specified day and at specified times. We might further specify the events and behaviors that we want caregivers to attend to. In some cases, you might even provide a list of terms for the recorder to use so that responses will be standardized across respondents. In Figure 2.3 we illustrate a diary form we use with adolescents to record incidents of aggression.

We have also used diaries with parents of kindergarteners to assess the variety of their literacy and play events in the home. Again, a certain

	Date	Homeroom

Who'd you talk with today and where'd you talk with them?

	Who	Where
1		
2		
3		
4		
5		

What did you do and say to them? (Use your Glossary!)

Did you hit or tease anyone? Who? How? (Use Glossary again)

Where'd this happen?
Why'd you do it?

About how many other kids were around?
Who?

Did anyone hit or tease you? Who? How? (Use Glossary again)

About how many kids were around?
Who?

How did you and they feel after?

Glossary: doing nothing/unoccupied, near but not with someone, talk, argue, tease, tease back, rough play, fight/hit, fight/hit back, sad, happy, hurt, gives up

Figure 2.3 Student diary page

day is specified and we ask caregivers to attend specifically to the places and participants in these events. A sample of this form is found in Figure 2.4. To maximize return rates with the diaries, which were sent out monthly across the school year, we paid caregivers for each diary returned. While we got a high return rate, we were not convinced that the data were efficacious. In some cases social desirability was evident (e.g. noting that the child read five books in one morning before going to school) and in other, more frequent cases, it seemed as though diary entries for more than one month were completed on one day.

Literacy journals (separate for each date)

Child's name: John
Date: 2-10-98

Participants*
David M. Schwart

Title of book 1   How Much is a Million

Genre picture non-fiction

Participants alone

Who wrote response John

Title of book 2

Genre

Participants

Who wrote response

Title of book 3

Genre

Participants

Who wrote response

etc.

* (e.g. alone, mother, father, grandma, grandpa, brother, sister, baby sitter, friend, specific other)

Figure 2.4 Literacy journal

A more successful procedure for securing valid diary data was to have diaries sent home as part of the child's school experience. In our study of social networks and first grade literacy (Pellegrini *et al.*, 1995a) the teacher (Betty Shockley) sent a book and a journal home with children three times per week across the whole school year. Children were expected to read and respond (e.g. write or draw a picture about the book), and record with whom they interacted during these home literacy events. Consequently, these journals provided an excellent record to the participants in children's home literacy events. Part of the success of this method was the teacher. The children and their caregivers had the greatest trust in and respect for Betty, thus they were willing to spend the time on the journals.

Analogue settings: direct

Analogue settings are constructed so as to resemble children's natural worlds, yet they are contrived so that variables can be controlled and manipulated. Analogue methods are used by researchers to overcome some of the sampling and standardization problems of naturalistic research. The observations can be carried out in the familiar setting of the child's home or, more typically, in a laboratory. In cases of analogue methods being used in the home, some amount of anxiety (on the part of both the child and the caregiver) should be reduced. Whether analogue methods are used in experimental laboratories or in the home, children and families must be given time to habituate to the situation. Thus, durations of events must be long enough to allow for habituation plus allow for a reasonable sampling of the behavior of interest. It is often best to conduct at least two observations per setting of interest and aggregate the data from those sessions. As this is basically an issue of sampling, reliability is increased with the number and duration of the observation periods.

Advantages

Since sampling relevant behavior in home visits using naturalistic and direct methods often means spending substantial periods of time in the home waiting for the event to occur, one benefit of contrived settings is efficiency. We could simply go into the home and construct and analogue situation and record it.

A second benefit of using analogue settings is standardization. By standardization we mean that the observation context is similar across all participants. So if we want to observe parent–child play or mother–child book reading we would provide a similar set of toys and books for the participants to interact with. In this way any differences in behavior due to materials is minimized. Examples for this approach abound. Brody and colleagues (1994) observed parent–child and peer interactions while children were playing a board game at home. Dickinson and colleagues observed parents and children at home after providing standardized books and play props (e.g. DeTemple and Beals, 1991; Dickinson *et al.*, 1992).

Disadvantages

The costs associated with collecting data in analogue settings, even when conducted in the home, are high and should be considered. As in all other forms of home observations, logistics are usually complicated. More relevant to the validity of the data collected, contrived tasks or settings can elicit unrepresentative behavior from participants. Issues such as participants' reactivity and the meaningfulness of the tasks to the participants are important. Reactivity can be addressed through repeated observations: repetition brings familiarity.

Task authenticity

Regarding meaningfulness of the task, tasks and materials used in elicitation contexts should be selected or designed as being representative of the sorts of tasks these participants might actually do at home, on their own. One strategy in designing an analogue setting is to observe the participants in their natural habit and determine the locations, props and people that typify literacy events. For example, in our study of Head Start mothers reading to their children (Pellegrini *et al.*, 1990) we found initially that neither mothers nor children were interested in the 'traditional' trade books read in many middle class homes (e.g. Beatrix Potter books). After spending time in the home and talking with mothers we found that mothers and their children often interacted around newspaper advertisements for toys and comics. Using these materials, we designed texts to be read in the home. This sort of experimental design is 'ecologically valid', according to Bronfennbrenner (1979).

When this sort of procedure is not followed, we typically underestimate the competence of those we are observing. When props and situations are unfamiliar or uninteresting, participants are not motivated to exhibit competence, especially in an assessment situation which can be intimidating under the best of circumstances. Unfortunate examples of this sort of mistake abound in the literature. For example, in studies of social class differences in mother–child play, researchers typically gave participants sets of toys to play with and gauged differences in competence by the level of symbolism observed in children's play (see McLoyd, 1980 and Rubin *et al.*, 1983 for informative critiques). The toys provided as props were those typically found in middle class homes; thus for middle class children and mothers these toys were more familiar than they were for lower socioeconomic status mothers and children. The play of the former group was judged to be more 'sophisticated' than that of the latter. Differences in observed 'sophistication' were probably due to differences in familiarity with the props. As props become familiar, interactions and play become more complex (Rubin *et al.*, 1983).

Analogue settings: indirect

Indirect methods applied to hypothetical situations are yet more removed from direct observations of children in their home situations. Because we did not use this sort of method in our projects we will present only a very brief description.

The sorts of methods included in this genre involve asking children and parents questions about hypothetical situations related to literacy. For example, Stanovich (1993) developed a measure of children's familiarity with a sample of children's books. The child is presented with a list containing titles of real children's books as well as distractor titles, or made-up titles. Children check off those titles they recognize and the researcher gains insight into their experience with books. Other examples might include questionnaires asking parents about their beliefs concerning the ways in which children develop (Pellegrini and Stanic, 1993) and inventories of children's reading preferences.

To conclude this section on studying children's literacy at home, we recognize the difficulty and expense involved in conducting direct observations of children in their homes. However, it may be more costly to *not* study children in their homes. Much of the data we have to date on children's home literacy events are derived from indirect and analogue methods. In some cases these data have led to incomplete and/or inaccurate descriptions of children and their families (particularly of those from culturally different groups). At a minimum it is useful to spend time in homes in order to understand the ecology of home literacy events. This information could then be used to design analogue situations or indirect measures of literacy events.

Children in schools

In this section we discuss methods used to study children in their school-based literacy events. Of prime concern to us was an accurate and full record of the oral language children used in these events. As part of understanding the meaning of this language, as well as factors influencing it, we also wanted to know about the context in which the language was generated. Our orientation toward language production is that the form of language used is influenced by the social and physical context in which the speaker is embedded.

Relevant aspects of the social context include the variety, number and relationships of participants in the discourse. For example, was the focal child talking to a teacher or a peer? Was the peer a friend? Concerning the physical context we were interested in the location within the classroom where the language was recorded. Was it while children were in a dramatic play context? Were the props in the context male or female preferred? Factors like these influence children's language and provide insight into their choices of language use.

Besides children's oral language, and the context in which it is embedded, we were also interested in children's reading and writing ability. As noted in Chapter 1, we considered children's ability to use 'literate language' as a developmental precursor to formal, school-based, reading and writing. In this section we also describe different measures of school-based literacy.

Naturalistic methods: direct

Direct naturalistic methods for studying children's school-based literacy present some of the same problems as does conducting research in the home. The problems of logistics and reactivity are all as relevant here as in the home. Solutions, too, are similar. Yet school-based research also presents some unique problems.

Gaining access

The first problem associated with conducting school-based research is gaining access to the schools. Schools are very busy places. They are also places under close public scrutiny. Consequently, they are often reluctant to admit researchers who might disrupt the normal flow of everyday events or in some way place schools at risk for public criticism. Thus to gain access a researcher often has to have something to offer the schools in return.

Most typically researchers offer schools financial reimbursement in exchange for participation. For example, in two of the studies reported in this book, we offered teachers an honorarium in exchange for their participation. We felt that a small financial reward was a fair exchange for the time teachers spent accommodating to our disruptions and for their spending time completing questionnaires on children. In other studies we have offered teachers and school librarians children's books as tokens of our appreciation for their participation in our research.

Schools are often particularly enthusiastic to participate in a project which they think will have a positive impact on education generally, and on their school particularly. So when we talked to principals about determining the effect of different school recess regimens on children's attention to school tasks, they were most eager to participate. For the work reported in this book, teachers and principals recognized the importance of forging a home–school connection so they were most eager to facilitate this. Further legitimacy was added to the project by the specific researchers. They were not only researchers but also parents of children in the school district and viewed by the schools as advocates.

Individual classroom teachers are also becoming more involved in research. Building up on the ideas presented a century ago by the British labor historian R. H. Tawney (Terrill, 1973) and the Gestalt psychologist K. Lewin (1946), the practice of action research is widely practiced in many North American schools. The basic idea behind action research is that teachers should study and research pedagogical problems in their classroom with the intention of using this knowledge to improve their lot and the lot of their pupils.

In our first grade study, one of the researchers, Betty Shockley, was also a teacher in one of the classrooms.

Reactivity

Having a teacher as member of the research team attenuates another problem, and one common to home studies as well, habituation. As we noted in the preceding section, children and parents must habituate to researchers' presence if we are to gather reliable and valid data. When participants have not habituated they may exhibit the sorts of behaviors they think researchers want to see or they may exhibit low levels of competence. Thus, teacher as researcher minimizes this problem. Children accept them as part of the classroom ecology.

In our studies of children in schools we tried to minimize our obtrusiveness in a number of additional ways. First, in our studies of first grade children in classroom literacy events, we as researchers were present in the classroom in the first week of school and one of us was in the classroom once per week until spring. During this time the researchers participated in the classroom routines (e.g. listening to children read) or were noninteractive observers. In other cases, researchers spent considerable time in the classrooms, mainly taking a participant role, before they began interacting with children as a data collector.

The problem of habituation is particularly relevant to one way in which we collected children's oral language. We wanted to get direct audio recordings of children's language as they interacted with peers and adults in their classrooms. To this end we outfitted children with individual audio recorders. For preschoolers we utilized wireless microphones (attached to a vest) which transmitted (via FM radio signals) to a receiver and an attached tape recorder. We were able to record multiple children simultaneously only by using microphones with *different* FM frequencies. In our first grade studies we had children wearing 'belly packs' containing a small audio recorder; attached to the recorder was a microphone which was attached to children's shirts. Procedurally, we had each child say his or her name and the date into the microphone upon putting on the equipment. In this way we had a 'voice print' of the child for coding.

Of course these microphones were quite novel for the children and they spent much time during the first one or two observations talking directly into the microphone, often repeating 'Hello my name is . . .'. With time, however, the apparatus was less novel and children went about their business after they said their names. We make this assumption because after the second or third observation some children started to use 'nasty language'; we assume they would not have used this sort of language if they were conscious of wearing the microphone.

Our observation procedure followed focal child sampling and continuous recording rules (Pellegrini, 1996). Specifically, individual children were observed, in counterbalanced order, and their language was recorded continuously for a specified time period. While children's language was being recorded a researcher also recorded the focal child's social contacts, indicating the identity of the children with whom the target interacted, and locations visited around the classroom. In other cases we had a researcher coding the level of children's play as well.

In these cases, the researcher utilized paper and pencil to record children's behavior. Thus, these two levels of direct recording provided a rather rich picture of children's language and the context in which it was generated.

A brief word should be said here about how oral language is treated once it was recorded. As you can imagine collecting samples of oral language from children across time resulted in a considerable amount of data. Researchers have a basic choice to make at this point (or actually at the point of project design): do they code from tapes directly or do they transcribe the whole tape and then code? Transcription is a massive undertaking given the ratio of about ten hours of transcription for every one hour of tape. Transcription makes sense only if researchers are inducing a coding system or are interested in extended discourse.

Analogue settings: direct

We constructed analogue situations of children's classroom experience because we were interested in controlling extraneous variables and manipulating theoretically relevant variables. Specifically we were interested in controlling variables that confounded the social groupings in which we observed children. For example, we wanted to control children's self-selection into certain peer groups or into specific classroom interest areas, or 'centers'. We also wanted to manipulate social and physical contexts to determine their effects. For example we were interested in the degree to which children used literate language with friends, compared to non-friends, because we observed, in naturalistic observations, that there was an association between friends being present and the occurrence of literate language.

To avoid some of the limitations of experiments discussed above we were careful to design ecologically valid experiments (Bronfenbrenner, 1979). For example, our observations of children in preschools and in primary schools indicated that during their free play time they interacted with children of the same gender and same race. Thus, in our analogues we approximated this by assigning children to groups of same gender and same race. Regarding expectations, we knew from our naturalistic observations in preschool and primary school classrooms that teachers assigned children to work in specific areas at certain times during the day. So we could also assign children to work in experimental groups and maintain the ecological validity of the analogues.

We had two general sorts of analogue settings. For our preschool experimental studies we observed children in an experimental playroom interacting with toys from their classrooms. In these cases children's behavior was videotaped through one-way viewing mirrors and tapes were subsequently coded. In the primary school experimental studies, children were taken into the hallways outside of their classrooms. Their language was recorded on hidden audio recorders and in some cases an experimenter, sitting at the table, coded children's social behavior.

Some of our primary school children were also asked to read and write in some experimental settings. In some cases a book was read to them and they were asked to write and talk about that book. Additionally, individual children were asked to re-read those books to the experimenter and their re-readings were audiotaped and coded, again, along a continuum approximating independent reading.

Analogue settings: indirect

These approaches to gaining insight into children's language and literacy are very common in many North American schools. They typically involve testing children to make inferences about their competence with language and in reading and writing. For example, children might be asked to read a standardized passage from a book, identify a series of vocabulary words and write all the words they know. In our work we complemented our more direct measures of language and literacy with their psychometric counterparts. In many cases this was done to establish the concurrent validity of our more direct measures. For example, we had direct measures of children's oral language (in both natural and analogue settings) where they talked about talk; for example, 'Doctors can't say poo poo'. We wanted to establish that these oral language measures were a measure of children's 'metalinguistic awareness', or the ability to think about language. To this end we administered measures of metalinguistic awareness (with established validity data), such as identifying which words rhyme, to children and correlated them with our measure of oral language.

In other cases we administered tests of reading and writing to children. Our measures of choice here were taken from Marie Clay's (1985) battery *Concepts about Print*. Again, we correlated these measures with our more direct measures of reading and writing.

Conclusion

Our intent in this chapter was to provide an introduction to the data collection procedures used in the studies contained in this book. Generally, we utilized a multi-method approach, using both naturalistic and experimental procedures. In our use of analogue procedures we always tried to design ecologically valid experiments. Specific details are presented with the individual studies.

Chapter 3

Joint reading between parents and children

Joint reading between mothers and their children enjoys a privileged place in the child language and the early literacy literatures. Caregivers interacting with very young children around texts of various sorts, but especially children's books, has been considered important in children's learning individual vocabulary words at least since the time of Werner and Kaplan (1952). More recently interest in the role of mother–child book reading in children's language learning was spurred by the work of Ninio and Bruner (1978; Ninio, 1980a, 1980b, 1983) and actively pursued by Snow (1983) and others (see Bus *et al.*, 1995 for review).

Mother–child book reading is also considered important in children's literacy learning. Indeed, it might be considered the paradigm early literacy event. Here children are 'actively' engaged in a social context where they are learning the social conventions of literacy in a highly enjoyable and aesthetic context (see Galda *et al.*, 1997; see also Cullinan and Galda, 1998). The importance assigned to early book reading for children's subsequent school-based literacy is obvious when one sees titles of journal articles such as 'What no bedtime story means' (Heath, 1982)!

The reading education literature, led by the pioneering work of Dolores Durkin (1966), stressed the importance of early book reading to children by demonstrating its importance in the lives of precocious young readers. Most recently the importance of joint book reading for learning to read in school was empirically verified in a meta-analysis of the literature conducted by Bus and colleagues (1995). In their findings book reading had an effect size of 0.59 and accounted for 8 percent of the variance in learning to read measures. Of equal importance was the finding that these effects were not dependent upon socioeconomic status.

The dimensions of book reading which are thought to be responsible for early literacy learning were succinctly presented by Teale (1984) when he suggested that joint book reading helped children recognize conventions of print (such as grapheme–phoneme relations) and that oral language can also be expressed in print.

Thus we have two literatures stressing the importance of parent–child reading for children's learning oral language and in becoming literate. In this chapter we present our research in the area of joint book reading and children's language and literacy learning.

Extending the social ecology of joint reading

Our research extends the traditional mother–child book reading literature in a number of important ways. First, concerning the caregivers, we examine the differential roles of mothers *and* fathers in joint book reading. To date, the vast majority of this literature has been concerned with mothers and children alone. Consideration of other caregivers, in addition to mothers, is crucial if we want to understand the social ecologies in which children actually live. The nuclear family in North America and much of Europe is changing rapidly. The increasing number of single-parent families means that children will probably experience a variety of caregivers in addition to mothers. We know, for example, that in many African American families maternal grandmothers play an important role in child rearing. At the same time, the role of fathers in many children's lives is increasingly important. Again, this is partially due to the changing structure of families where it is more common now, than in the recent past, for North American fathers, after a divorce, to have either joint or sole custody of their children. Given these demographic realities it is crucial to study fathers reading to their children. In the first study presented in this chapter we compare mothers and fathers in joint book reading contexts with their preschool age children.

The role of the child

Another common limitation of the extant literature in joint reading is that it for the most part presents a unidirectional model of parents (mostly mothers) socializing children. Little or no consideration is given to the child's contribution to the situation. From our knowledge of the broader literature on mother–child interaction (e.g. Bell, 1979) we know that child-level characteristics influence mothers' behaviors with children. Interactions between mothers and children then are more like transactions, where each participant contributes to the situation. Given this notion of social interaction, studies of parent–child book reading should consider, first, the degree to which parents accommodate to children's individual differences, and second, how this is done.

In the first study presented in this chapter, we examine how mothers and fathers accommodate to one sort of individual difference in children (communication disorders).

Theoretical orientation

The three studies presented in this chapter are guided by Vygotsky's (1962, 1978) theory that executive cognitive processes, such as monitoring and regulating behavior and cognitive processes, originate in the social interaction between children and significant adults, typically caregivers. The notion that higher cognitive processes move from the interpsychological plane to the intra-psychological plane has been convincingly argued by Wertsch and colleagues (Wertsch, 1979; Wertsch *et al.*, 1980). The process by which this internalization occurs involves caregivers structuring interaction around tasks in such a way as to maximize children's participation in those events.

Initially this may mean that parents must make few cognitive demands on the child and provide a fair amount of structure for children so that they can participate in the task. For example, asking a child a yes/no question is low in demand but high on structure. Most children should be able to participate in this level of interaction.

With increased skills and as children are more capable of taking over task responsibilities, parents can be more demanding and provide less support for their participation. For example, a mother might ask a child open-ended questions (low on structure) which ask a child to generalize (high on cognitive demand). This sort of dialogic strategy facilitates the gradual appropriation of task responsibility such that children internalize the rules and roles characteristic of reading. This process was labeled by Vygotsky (1978) as teaching within the child's zone of proximal development.

We extend Vygotsky's analysis by proposing that these dialogue strategies for literacy can be learned effectively in the joint book reading context. They are then taken by children and used with their peers in pretend play. Following Piaget's notion of play as practice we will propose and demonstrate in later chapters that the pretend tenor of peer play enables children to master the use of literate language in that both social fantasy and early literacy events share a number of important design features. Subsequently, children use literate language with their peers and adults in the realistic context of school literacy events.

This model that we present is both hypothetical and in need of extensive longitudinal testing. Even with support, it would be only a description of one of many developmental trajectories by which children become literate. Other children may become literate with limited book reading experiences with parents (as seems to be the case with Japanese children: Stevenson and Lee, 1990) or with limited fantasy experiences.

Study I: different types of children with mothers and fathers

In this work we (Pellegrini *et al.*, 1985a) tried to document the ways in which mothers and fathers, while reading with their preschool children, taught within the zone of proximal development. We examined parental interaction with two types of children: communicatively handicapped (CH) and non communicatively handicapped (NHC). By studying parental interactions with these two groups of children we hoped to gain insight into the extent to which children themselves contributed to the interaction process.

We were concerned with the degree to which each parent's verbal and nonverbal behaviors with their CH and NHC children were more or less supportive as a function of children's age and communicative status. We hypothesized that parents would be more demanding and less supportive with more competent children than with less competent children. The model further hypothesizes that children use these dialogue strategies independently in similar tasks. We were also interested in the degree to which these different interaction variables related to a global measure of children's language, verbal IQ.

This study complemented the extant literature in a number of important ways. Our choice to study children from 3- to 5-years-of-age extends the age range of earlier studies, most of which looked at mothers reading to children from $1\frac{1}{2}$-years-of-age to 3-years-of-age (Anderson *et al.*, 1980; DeLoach and Mendoza, 1987). Our empirical work with children's private speech suggested that the internalization of speech processes continued throughout the preschool period (Pellegrini, 1981). We hypothesized that each parent would be more directive and supportive as well as less demanding with younger children compared to older children.

While children's age is a proxy for their level of competence, their ability to communicate with parents is a much more direct measure of competence in a task which is dependent upon verbal interaction. Parents speak differently to CH children, compared to NCH children (Crambit and Siegel, 1977; Leonard, 1982). Adults talk to CH children in much the same way as they do to younger NCH children: they use simple syntax and few lexical items. More important to our hypothesis, parents of CH, compared to NCH, children seem to make fewer cognitive demands on the children (Crambit and Siegel, 1977).

The mental demand associated with the coding of the contents of these categories was derived from Sigel's Distancing Hypothesis (Sigel and McGillicuddy-DeLisi, 1984) whereby adults can facilitate children's cognitive development by engaging them in specific forms of dialogue. The aim of these dialogue strategies was to help children put cognitive distance between the stimuli and themselves, resulting in children's cognitive representations. Low mental demand strategies included asking children to label or describe a picture or to reproduce an utterance. Medium mental demands had children sequencing events, inferring similarities and differences, and classifying. High mental demands included evaluations, inferring cause and effect, generalizing and resolving conflicts.

Method

The families involved in this study were part of a larger project directed by Irving Sigel at Educational Testing Service, Princeton (see Pellegrini *et al.*, 1985a, 1985b for more details). Participants in this study included 120 families (60 CH and 60 NCH). Families were generally of high social economic status.

The CH sample was identified by a speech pathologist as having language production problems or delays. The two samples were matched in terms of children's age, gender, ordinal position in the family and parents' level of education. CH and NCH children were grouped into a younger group (M = 49-months) or an older group (M = 62-months).

Procedurally, the Wechsler Preschool and Primary Scales of Intelligence (WPPSI: Wechsler, 1974) were administered to each child. The children were read stories (*Hello Rock*, by R. Bradfield, and *A Rainbow of My Own*, by D. Freeman) by mother and father. These sessions were videotaped and coded directly from the tapes. To sample teaching strategies at the beginning, middle and end of sessions, only the first and last two minutes as well as the mid one minute of the tapes were coded.

Parents' behaviors were coded according to form (statement or question), verbal emotional direction (e.g. Good) and disapproval (e.g. No, that's wrong), nonverbal direction/support (e.g. patting a child to soothe him or her; turning a page for a child) and content of the utterances (high, medium and low mental demands). Conversational turns between child and parent were also coded.

Results/discussion

The descriptive statistics for the interaction measures are displayed in Table 3.1.

Differences associated with parents

Regarding differences between parents, we found virtually no differences between mothers' and fathers' language with their children. This finding is somewhat at odds with theory and data presented by Block (1983) who suggested that fathers, compared to mothers, were more demanding, especially with their sons.

This discrepancy with Block's model may be due to a number of factors. First, Block's data were collected in more naturalistic contexts than ours. Thus, our parents may have been 'performing' in the experimental setting. Relatedly, the naturalistic setting may have confounded parental role and activity. Parents may have chosen to interact with their children in those settings which maximize these differences. Self-selection differences, of course, are controlled in experimental studies. Certainly more research is needed to resolve this sort of discrepancy.

Differences associated with children

The analysis of variance (ANOVA) summary table for the effects of communicative status is presented in Table 3.2. Additionally, correlations coefficients between interaction variables and children's age and IQ, by age and communicative status, are presented in Table 3.1.

That parents used more directive and supportive strategies with younger and CH children was only partially supported. Parents' use of high and medium demand strategies did not vary according to

Table 3.1 Correlation coefficients between children's age and parent interaction variables for each group of children

	4-year-olds				5-year-olds				Total			
	NCH		CH		NCH		CH		NCH		CH	
Variables	Age	IQ	Age	IQ	Age	IQ	Age	IQ	Age	IQ	Age	IQ
Statements	−0.22	0.006	−0.05	−0.14	−0.02	−0.08	−0.17	−0.16	−0.08	0.04	−0.19	−0.10
Questions	−0.32	−0.03	−0.14	−0.23	0.11	−0.02	−0.02	0.08	−0.06	−0.09	−0.14	−0.06
Verbal/emotional support	0.01	0.04	−0.10	0.46**	0.19	0.15	0.02	0.25	0.05	0.04	−0.26**	0.26
Nonverbal management	−0.35	−0.22	−0.01	−0.14	0.03	−0.52**	−0.14	−0.21	−0.10	−0.20	−0.28	0.25*
High demand	−0.30	0.24	0.12	−0.06	0.20	0.51**	0.18	−0.01	−0.02	0.16	0.08	0.13
Medium demand	−0.25	−0.002	0.03	−0.15	0.18	−0.12	−0.21	0.26	−0.06	−0.02	−0.11	−0.57**
Low demand	−0.02	−0.40*	−0.25	0.39*	−0.08	−0.68**	−0.32	−0.08	−0.05	−0.34**	−0.38**	−0.30*
Paraphrasing	0.01	0.01	0.07	0.27	−0.35	0.09	−0.08	−0.18	−0.03	0.21	0.31*	0.22
Turns	−0.19	−0.40*	0.07	−0.20	−0.03	0.21	−0.24	−0.007	−0.15	−0.33**	−0.32**	−0.18

Notes

CH = communicatively handicapped; NCH = non communicatively handicapped. df = 28 for each age group; 58 for total.

*p<0.05; **p<0.01

Table 3.2 Frequencies for parental interaction variables by children's age and communicative status

Variables	Communicative status				
	Communicatively handicapped		Non communicatively handicapped		
	M	SD	M	SD	F^a
4-year-olds					
Statements	19.67	8.55	19.47	7.39	0.41*
Questions	28.80	10.90	26.69	9.69	3.49*
Verbal/emotional support	10.83	5.14	10.11	4.98	0.05*
Nonverbal management	19.27	12.15	18.52	14.62	2.13*
High demand	16.88	7.89	18.40	7.08	2.29*
Medium demand	3.41	2.91	3.54	2.73	0.07*
Low demand	32.53	14.69	25.20	9.64	20.10**
Paraphrasing	68.20	31.25	79.16	29.66	14.73**
Turns	76.43	18.45	70.50	15.58	7.10**
5-year-olds					
Statements	19.18	8.86	17.52	8.01	
Questions	28.53	10.28	25.18	7.80	
Verbal/emotional support	9.89	5.37	8.66	4.21	
Nonverbal management	18.29	15.98	11.81	10.78	
High demand	16.68	7.41	18.45	7.73	
Medium demand	3.22	2.62	3.20	2.31	
Low demand	31.67	14.92	20.62	8.15	
Paraphrasing	71.15	29.50	94.35	22.30	
Turns	72.51	19.75	62.39	16.17	

Notes
a df = 1.119
* $p < 0.05$
** $p < 0.01$

children's age or CH status. This may have been due to the relative simplicity of the books chosen. We know, and will see later in this chapter, that different books, such as books written in different genres, elicit different interaction strategies. Parents did, however, use more low demand strategies with CH children, compared to NCH children. Correlations between use of low demand strategies and age, within the CH group, show a negative correlation with age: use decreased with age only for CH children.

There was also a greater frequency of conversational turns observed between CH children and their parents. This may indicate that parents are trying to involve children in the conversation by trying to elicit children's language.

Parental strategies and children's verbal IQ

When we look at the relation between parents' interaction strategies and children's verbal IQ a clearer picture begins to emerge. With IQ as a criterion variable, we constructed separate regression models for CH and NCH children and allowed all of our interaction measures to enter freely. Summaries for these regression models are presented in Table 3.3.

Different interaction strategies predicted IQ for the CH and NCH children. For the CH children low cognitive demand strategies and questions were both positive and significant predictors. For the NCH children, on the other hand, high cognitive demands were positive predictors and questions were negative predictors. These results are consistent with the Vygotskian model of parents using low demand strategies to engage less competent children in a task and high demand strategies to engage more competent children.

These results are interesting from both pedagogical and theoretical perspectives. First, in terms of pedagogy the use of high mental demand strategies is not something teachers should *always* aim for. There are

Table 3.3 Stepwise regression analyses for parental predictors of children's IQ by communicative status

Variable entered[a]	R^2	df	F	B value
NCH children				
High cognitive demand	0.49	1,59	27.61*	0.52
Questions	0.53	2,59	9.42*	−0.34
CH children				
Verbal support	0.19	1,59	13.72*	0.88
Low cognitive demand	0.24	2,59	8.96*	0.20
Questions	0.27	3,59	6.89	0.22

Notes
NCH = non communicatively handicapped; CH = communicatively handicapped
[a]Only variables meeting the 0.05 significance level were entered into the model
*$p<0.01$

instances when we merely want a strategy to involve children in discourse around a task; we do not want strategies which are too challenging for children or strategies which provide us with great insight into children's cognitive competence. In these cases low, not high, mental demand strategies should be used.

At the level of theory, it becomes interesting to determine the point in discourse when high demand strategies are used relative to low demand strategies. Do parents start off with high strategies, giving children an opportunity to 'show their stuff' and continue high if children meet the challenge? If children do not meet the challenge, then do parents use lower mental demand strategies? This sequential approach to analyzing the interactions around book reading is necessary in order to understand the impact of these strategies on children's performance and the impact of children's performance on the use of these strategies. Our analysis techniques should approximate the world of the people we study. Neither children nor parents produce and comprehend individual utterances, independent of antecedent and consequential utterances. We take this approach in Study 2.

Study 2: working class mothers reading with their children

The majority of mother–child book reading studies involve mothers from middle or upper social economic groups. The parents in Study 1, for example, were highly educated adults living in the vicinity of Princeton, NJ. The wider research literature finds, as we did in Study 1, that middle class (MC) parents (mostly mothers) do demonstrate teaching strategies that are sensitive to children's levels of competence and consistent with Vygotsky's notion of the zone of proximal development. These parental tutorials are often held up as powerful predictors of children's subsequent school-based literacy. By implication, the lack of parent–child book reading is often proffered as an explanation for the poor performance of lower socioeconomic status (LSES) children in school (Ogbu, 1981).

Social class differences in book reading behavior

In cases where LSES mothers and their children have been observed in joint reading events (e.g. Ninio, 1980a) it was found that their interaction strategies were not as effective as those used by MC mothers.

We suggest that some of the observed class differences observed in these studies of mother–child book reading are artifacts of the experimental situations in which mothers and their children were observed. Specifically, part of the reason for MC mothers' relative superiority in joint book reading was due to their being more familiar with the type of books than their LSES counterparts.

An analogous situation existed in much of the research into class differences in mother–child play. In this literature, like in the mother–child book reading literature, MC, compared to LSES, mothers were shown to have played with their children in more sophisticated ways and their children, in turn, exhibited higher levels of play. The toys used in these laboratory studies of play, like the books used in laboratory studies of book reading, are more familiar to MC mothers and children than to LSES mothers and children. This familiarity allows mothers and children alike to exhibit sophisticated language forms.

In our study we tested this proposition experimentally by observing LSES mothers and their children interacting with familiar format texts and unfamiliar format texts. High levels of competence should be exhibited in the former compared to the latter condition. We defined competence in terms of mothers' adjusting the cognitive demands of their language to children's level of performance. For example, if children respond appropriately to a high mental demand strategy, mothers should follow with another high demand strategy. If children respond inappropriately, mothers should use a less demanding strategy. Again, the mother should be maximizing children's participation in the book reading process. This level of analysis should provide a more direct test of Vygotsky's theory of the zone of proximal development. As noted above, such a direct test would involve a sequential analysis of the language used by mothers and children.

Beginning of literate language

Another dimension of Vygotsky's theory, and one particularly important for education, is the degree to which these strategies used between mothers and children are then used by children in school-based literacy events. As a first step toward answering these questions we wanted to identify the extent to which oral language precursors to school-based literacy originated in mother–child book reading discourse. Indeed one of the proposed functions that early book reading serves is that it exposes children to the language forms used by teachers (Cook-Gumperz, 1982) and in the books which are used in school-based literacy events (Anderson *et al.*, 1980).

Children's ability to talk about language and print is one particularly important form of language that predicts early reading (Pellegrini and Galda, 1991). The ability to talk about language and literacy, as we and others (Olson, 1977) have argued, is an indicator of children's ability to reflect upon the language and literacy systems. Children's ability to reflect upon language is one of the more robust predictors of early school-based literacy (Adams, 1990). We were interested in the degree to which children were exposed to this 'metalanguage' in joint book reading events.

Our developmental model posits that children are first exposed systematically to 'literate language', of which metalanguage is an important component during joint reading. Children then take these newly learned forms and practice them in play with their peers and eventually use them in realistic school-based literacy events.

The importance of literary genre

We also recognized that not all texts that children and mothers read would elicit metalanguage. As part of a discussion with colleagues after a symposium on book reading, one noted scholar bemoaned the fact that children in her studies were not generating narrative during book reading sessions. One of us responded that it was not a surprise since the mothers weren't reading narratives, but rather were reading expository texts! At that point we recognized the potential importance of different literary genres in the sorts of language that mothers and children generate around those books.

In this study we experimentally manipulated the literary genres. Narrative and expository texts were used in both familiar formats (narratives were newspaper cartoons and expositories were toy advertisements) and traditional formats (children's books in the narrative and expository modes). We hypothesized that the expository, compared to the narrative, texts lent themselves more readily to teaching and reflection upon language. These texts, most typically represented by alphabet and animal books, are not written with story lines; individual bits of information are present as pictures and accompanying texts.

Thus to keep children engaged with the text, mothers must talk about the text and the pictures. With narratives, the story line usually keeps children engaged. The sorts of talk used in expository text, we figured, would resemble teaching, by asking children to identify, label, and talk about pictures and words in the book. We also thought that

LSES mothers would be most facile around familiar, compared to traditional, format texts.

Method

The data from this study were part of a larger study of mother–child book reading (Pellegrini *et al.*, 1990) among LSES families. In this study we were particularly interested in LSES African American mothers and their children (three girls and ten boys with a mean age of 52-months), who were enrolled in a Head Start program in Athens, GA, USA.

As part of this project we enrolled thirteen families for a series of extended observations where we would observe mothers interacting with their children at home. Parents were recruited with the help of a local Head Start program that was interested in strengthening home–school relations and children's early literacy experiences. The Head Start director arranged a parents' meeting one evening which we attended. At that meeting we explained that we were interested in helping children learn to become successful readers and writers in school and part of this program was to study the ways in which parents read to their children at home. We also explained that we would be designing teaching strategies to be used at home and at school based on our observations. We then asked for volunteers and offered to pay them $40 in exchange for participation.

In the initial home observations, a research associate, who was also a former preschool teacher, visited the home and interviewed mothers. As part of this process the observer completed the HOME Inventory (Caldwell and Bradley, 1984). From the HOME interview we recognized that most families had few if any children's books in the home but all families received at home a free local newspaper that contained some news and a few cartoons, but was mostly advertisements. From this newspaper we constructed two narrative (cartoons) and two expository (advertisements) texts for mothers and children to read. These were labeled familiar format texts. We also presented mothers and children with two traditional narratives (*Peter Rabbit* and the *Little Red Hen*) and two expository texts (*Who Lives in the Zoo* and *My First Book of Words*).

Mothers and children were observed in their homes as they read these texts, in counterbalanced order, with their children. These sessions were videotaped, transcribed and coded using codes similar to those used in Study 1, where utterances were categorized in terms of high, medium and low mental demands. We also coded mothers' uses of metalinguistic verbs, or verbs which encoded some aspect of the linguistic process, for example, '**Say** that again'.

We also coded children's behaviors so that we could construct an interactive picture of book-reading episodes. Children's utterances were coded in terms of initiations, e.g. a question, which were not in direct response to the mother's immediately preceding utterance. Children's responses to mothers' utterances were coded as being relevant to the text (e.g. child talks about a picture in the text) or relevant to extra-textual phenomena (e.g. child relates mother's utterance to the outside world, 'We have a cat too').

These child level codes were indicative of children's level of task participation. Initiations by children, in comparison to responses, were indicative of higher levels of task competence. This conceptualization is consistent with the use of the zone of proximal development as an assessment construct. Assessment of children's level of competence in a task, according to the zone of proximal development, should be gauged by the amount of parent support required to involve children in the task. Competence, then, is judged by level of task participation, not by an outcome related, or test-like, measure of children's performance on the task. In Study 3 we present results on these more psychometrically oriented measures.

In coding both child and maternal utterances, the integrity of the order of the utterances was retained. So the order of mother and child utterances, as they actually appeared on the tapes, was maintained. This strategy, as cumbersome as it was, was necessary to conduct sequential analyses of the interactions. Our aim was to analyze utterances as they naturally occurred.

Results/discussion

Genre and format effects

Summaries of the ANOVAs and mean values for the effect of text on mothers' teaching strategies are presented in Table 3.4. Summaries and mean values for the effects on children's levels of participation are presented in Table 3.5.

Main effects for genre were found. Mothers and children talked more and used more of each of the coded categories around expository texts, compared to narrative texts. This should be of no surprise. Narratives, good ones at least, are written in such a way as to engage the reader/

Table 3.4 Summary results for the effects of text condition on mothers' teaching strategies

Teaching strategies comparison	F	p	Means for each text[a]				
			1	2	3	4	Multiple
Low mental demand	9.99	0.0009	0.04	0.12	0.13	0.02	2 >4,3 >4
Medium mental demand	5.85	0.002	0.10	0.17	0.18	0.04	2 >4,3 >4
High mental demand	10.54	0.0005	0.03	0.07	0.09	0.01	2 >4,3 >4
Metalinguistic terms	0.395	NS	0.001	0.002	0.003	0.007	NS

Notes
a df = 3,36
1 = traditional narrative, 2 = traditional expository, 3 = familiar expository, 4 = familiar narrative

Table 3.5 Summary results for the effects of text condition on children's task participation behavior

Children's participation	F	p	Means for each text[a]				
			1	2	3	4	Multiple
Initiations	4.04	0.01	14.08	19.38	23.23	4.46	3>4, 2>4
Book-relevant responses	12.73	0.0001	8.69	59.61	50.46	6.0	2>4, 3>4
Text-external reference	2.90	0.04	0.69	3.62	8.38	0.15	2>4, 3>4

Notes
a df = 3,36
1 = traditional narrative, 2 = traditional expository, 3 = familiar expository, 4 = familiar narrative

listener. The narrative line should engulf the reader's attention in such a way that maternal comments on the text actually *distract* children from the text. How often have overly didactic parents been reminded by their children during bed time stories to just read the book and stop asking questions!

With expository texts, on the other hand, there is no such engaging story line. A series of loosely related items is presented and parental teaching strategies are needed to center children's attention. This can be done by interrelating the separate items into a narrative-line presentation. Alternatively, mother and children can relate the items in the text to similar items in their own worlds. For these reasons it seems to us that expository, compared to narrative, texts might be more useful in didactic school lessons.

Next we consider the maternal strategies which related to children's participation in the task. Because of the genre differences we analyzed only expository texts.

Initial analyses were conducted to determine the effects of format within the expository genre on interaction patterns. At one, simple, level, we found no effects for text format (traditional vs familiar) on the frequency with which mothers and children used specific interaction categories. This level of interaction was too simple for detecting differences in mothers' teaching strategies.

We used maternal utterances to predict children's level of participation in the expository texts in both formats. Summaries of the regression models for traditional and familiar expository texts, respectively, are displayed in Tables 3.6 and 3.7. Generally, mothers used more demanding strategies to involve children in the familiar text tasks than in the traditional text tasks. When we examine children's use of initiations and children's reference to stimuli external to the texts as measures of task participation, we found that maternal use of high mental demand strategies and metalinguistic terms predicted initiations. With traditional texts, on the other hand, medium demand strategies by mothers were predictive.

When we consider children's responses to mothers with task relevant responses, indicative of a relatively low level of task participation, we found mothers using similar strategies in both traditional and familiar formats. In both cases mothers used both high and medium demand strategies.

These results indicate that children, and probably mothers as well, were more competent around the familiar texts, compared to the traditional, and consequently exhibited higher levels of task participation.

Table 3.6 Summary of regression analyses for maternal strategies relating to children's participation around traditional expository texts

Participation measures and maternal strategies	Step	R^2	B value	F	p
Initiations:					
Low demand	0.1	0.70	0.16	25.64	0.0004
Book relevant:					
Medium demand	0.1	0.91	0.14	6.5	0.03
Metalinguistic	0.2	0.94	4.9	3.11	0.11
Vocabulary × metalinguistic	0.3	0.96	0.4	3.77	0.09
High demand	0.4	0.98	1.16	8.23	0.02
External reference:					
Medium	0.1	0.71	0.02	26.94	0.0003

Table 3.7 Summary of regression analyses for maternal strategies relating to children's participation around familiar expository texts

Participation measures and maternal strategies	Step	R^2	B value	F	p
Initiations:					
Metalinguistic	0.1	0.61	3.05	17.53	0.001
High demand	0.2	0.69	0.19	11.32	0.002
Book relevant:					
High demand	0.1	0.56	0.01	14.07	0.003
Vocabulary ×					
low demand	0.2	0.76	0.0002	8.23	0.01
External reference:					
Metalinguistic	0.1	0.66	1.97	21.77	0.0007
Vocabulary ×					
high demand	0.2	0.91	−0.002	27.97	0.0004
Vocabulary ×					
metalinguistic	0.3	0.96	0.04	11.92	0.007

Maternal sensitivity to children's responses

An important dimension of the zone of proximal development is that maternal interaction/teaching styles will be sensitive to children's levels of performance in the task. Mothers' strategies should be gauged to children's immediate performance. We examined the degree to which mothers adjusted their strategies to children's performance by testing the following mother (M)–child (C) sequential probability:

M: high demand-> C: no response -> M: medium demand

The probability of this sequence occurring was tested, following procedures outlined by Bakeman and Gottman (1986). This was accomplished by identifying all utterances following the above sequence. We then tested whether these sequences occurred at a greater than chance probability in both traditional and familiar expository conditions. The probability was beyond chance level in both formats.

Another measure of maternal sensitivity to children's performance was the degree to which mothers' use of interaction strategies interacted with children's vocabulary level, as indicated by the Peabody Picture Vocabulary Test (PPVT). We found that mothers' use of high mental demand strategies and metalinguistic terms interacted significantly with PPVT scores in predictions of children's task participation (where children make references external to the text) in the familiar format context only; these data are presented in Tables 3.8 and 3.9.

Table 3.8 Descriptive statistics for mothers' and children's utterances by text format

	Traditional text (TT)		Familiar text (FT)	
	M	SD	M	SD
Child				
Acknowledge	0.01	0.01	0.02	0.03
Ask question	0.01	0.02	0.02	0.02
Clarify	0.01	0.01	0.00	0.01
Conceptual conflict/disagree	0.02	0.03	0.02	0.02
Correct answer (subordinate)	0.08	0.10	0.16	0.13
Correct answer (superordinate)	0.03	0.04	0.05	0.05
Correct answer (other)	0.06	0.13	0.07	0.07
Inadequate answer	0.02	0.03	0.02	0.05
'Don't know'	0.01	0.01	0.02	0.02
Describes subordinate	0.02	0.03	0.02	0.03
Describes superordinate	0.01	0.01	0.00	0.00
Expands/extends	0.01	0.01	0.00	0.01
Initiates (subordinate)	0.05	0.06	0.06	0.05
Initiates (superordinate)	0.01	0.01	0.01	0.01
Linguistic	0.02	0.03	0.03	0.03
Narrativizes	0.01	0.01	0.00	0.00
Not relevant	0.50	0.40	0.29	0.25
Reads	0.01	0.01	0.01	0.01
Repeats	0.10	0.11	0.08	0.13
Text–world	0.01	0.01	0.01	0.02
'Want'	0.01	0.01	0.02	0.03
World–text	0.01	0.01	0.01	0.02
Total utterances	144.29	157.69	69.70	72.52
Mother				
Answers own questions	0.02	0.03	0.04	0.04
Describes action	0.01	0.02	0.01	0.01
Clarify	0.01	0.01	0.01	0.02
Conflict/disagree	0.01	0.01	0.01	0.01
Corrects	0.02	0.02	0.01	0.01
Asks for description	0.02	0.05	0.01	0.01
Asks for a label	0.02	0.04	0.01	0.02
Asks to read or spell	0.01	0.01	0.01	0.01
Asks about a subordinate	0.01	0.01	0.01	0.01
Asks about a superordinate	0.01	0.01	0.01	0.01

Table 3.8 Continued

	Traditional text (TT)		Familiar text (FT)	
	M	SD	M	SD
Describes	0.05	0.05	0.07	0.07
Gives superordinate label	0.02	0.02	0.04	0.03
Gives subordinate label	0.34	0.37	0.12	0.16
Expands child's utterance	0.01	0.01	0.01	0.01
Linguistic question	0.05	0.05	0.11	0.11
Narrativizes	0.01	0.02	0.01	0.01
Negative reinforcement	0.01	0.01	0.01	0.01
Orient	0.01	0.01	0.01	0.02
Reads present text	0.12	0.32	0.03	0.06
Reinforce/repeat	0.07	0.06	0.09	0.05
Slot/frame provided	0.01	0.02	0.01	0.02
Text–world	0.01	0.02	0.03	0.03
Wh-question	0.14	0.14	0.28	0.20
World–text	0.00	0.00	0.00	0.00
Yes/no question	0.01	0.01	0.01	0.01
Total utterances	191.94	183.72	109.70	105.41

Note
Figures are reported as proportions.

It may be the case that mothers' ability to involve children of different levels at this rather sophisticated level may have been supported by the familiar format condition. Mothers' use of strategies interacted with PPVT in both formats *only* when children's level of task participation was at a rather low level (responding relevantly to mothers' preceding utterances).

Thus mothers adjusted their teaching styles to children's ability to meet those demands in both conditions. Importantly these results show that LSES African American mothers, like their MC counterparts, do this. Thus reported SES and race differences in previous studies of book reading may have been due to methodological problems, such as a limited number of observations or observations being conducted in laboratories rather than homes. Certainly the books used by the experimenters also had an effect. That some researchers did not even report the book used in their experiments illustrates the low level of importance they assigned to them. Certainly future research must attend to both genre and familiarity issues.

LSES mothers are clearly competent teachers of their children when

Table 3.9 Correlations among maternal and child utterances and word learning and vocabulary measures

	Traditional text PPVT	Familiar text PPVT	Traditional text words	Familiar text words
Maternal				
Asks label	0.17	0.18	0.37	0.40*
Asks subordinate	0.27	0.38	0.08	0.47**
Asks superordinate	−0.01	0.20	−0.20	0.23
Expands	0.52**	0.63***	0.56**	0.48**
Linguistic	0.59***	0.22	0.60**	0.30
Text–world	0.42*	0.36	0.46*	0.38
World–text	0.00	−0.17	0.00	−0.35
Child				
Linguistic	0.36	0.27	0.14	0.24
Correct subordinate	0.47**	0.27	0.46*	0.33
Correct superordinate	0.32	0.06	−0.12	0.34
Initiate subordinate	0.30	0.05	0.29	−0.33
Initiate superordinate	0.47**	0.02	0.20	−0.31
Text–world	−0.30	0.05	−0.42*	−0.04
World–text	0.63***	0.15	0.65***	0.03

Notes
*$p<0.10$; **$p<0.05$; ***$p<0.01$

they interact around familiar format texts. This finding, however, was made clear only when we examined sequences of utterances used by mothers and children. In the next study we will examine the ways in which specific sequences of utterances relate to another dimension of children's performance in a book reading task: vocabulary development.

Another important feature of the next study is that it presents data on the interrelations between maternal utterances and children's use of linguistic terms.

Study 3: learning vocabulary in the context of joint reading

Following the traditions of Werner and Kaplan (1952), we examined the ways in which mothers facilitated children's vocabulary growth in joint reading events. Utilizing a LSES sample (part of whom were examined in Study 2: see p. 46), we examined vocabulary development at proximal and distal levels. Proximally, children's vocabulary was assessed in terms of their identifying words previously presented in the book which they were read. Distally, vocabulary was assessed by the PPVT, a global measure of receptive vocabulary.

Our coding of maternal and child language was guided by extant theory and research which suggests that vocabulary is developed when children attend to new words and talk about them.

At the most general level we examined a maternal strategy, expansions, which maximized children's talk. Expansions involve a mother repeating the child's utterance, e.g. 'Funny!', and then providing an opportunity for the child to talk more by expanding that utterance, e.g. 'Funny? Why do you think he's funny?'

Repeating the child's utterance serves a reinforcement function and encourages subsequent participation. The expansion then exposes the child to more language and then provides an explicit opportunity to use that new language as it relates to the child's own language. Expansions have been shown to facilitate many aspects of children's language, such as syntax (Cazden, 1965) and vocabulary growth (Dickinson and Smith, 1994).

Two other strategies are directly relevant to children's vocabulary development: text–world and world–text links (Cochran-Smith, 1984). These strategies are similar to the extent that they both have children interrelating aspects of the text to aspects of their personal worlds. With text–world strategies, information presented in the text is then extended to the world external to the text. For example, a mother reads 'Giraffe'. The child responds: 'We saw one at the zoo'. With world–text utterances, the external world is related to the text; for example, a child says 'Stumpy' (the name of the child's dog). Mother then says, 'Here's a puppy just like Stumpy', pointing to a picture in the book.

Lastly, we consider the use of linguistic terms. We have stressed the importance of linguistic terms as an indicator of metalinguistic awareness and subsequent school-based literacy. In Studies 1 and 2 we showed that parents used these terms in the course of interacting with their children around text. In this study we show the maternal utterances which relate to children's use of these terms. We suggest that children learn these terms in such literacy events.

One level of analysis involves presenting correlation coefficients between children's use of linguistic terms and mothers' language. Given the bi-directionality of correlation coefficients it is impossible to know if maternal utterances are antecedents or consequences of children's uses of linguistic terms. Thus, we also present sequential lag analyses whereby we examine the maternal antecedents to children's use of linguistic terms.

Method

The participants and procedures for this study were the same as for Study 2. Indeed the participants in Study 2 represented a subset of those examined here (see Pellegrini, *et al.*, 1995b); there were eight girls and eleven boys with a mean age of 51-months. There are only two procedural differences between Studies 2 and 3. First, the thirteen participants in Study 2 were all Head Start children (4-years-of-age) and their mothers were thus all SES; unlike Study 3 they were not all African American. Second, we utilized different coding systems. As noted in the introduction to this study, we coded maternal expansions as well as text–world and world–text utterances. Additionally, we coded mothers' and children's repetitions of preceding utterances (of the other speaker), asking for and giving labels (of pictures presented in the texts), mothers' Wh-questions and children's correct and incorrect responses to questions.

As in Study 2 we examined interactions around traditional and familiar expository texts. Immediately after children were read the individual texts, a researcher then asked them a series of word identification questions using words taken directly from the texts just read. Ten pictures were presented to the children after each of the four texts (two familiar and two traditional) and the children were asked: 'What's this?' The mean of the two familiar and the mean of the two traditional assessments were the units of analyses for the proximal measures. For the distal measures the children's standard score from the PPVT was used.

Results/discussion

Descriptive statistics for maternal and child utterances are displayed in Tables 3.10, 3.11 and 3.12. First, we found that mothers, compared to children, did most of the talking with both familiar and traditional books. This, of course, is not surprising. Mothers are the experts in these tasks for young children and they guide the interaction. It is the maternal language which becomes the stuff of children's literate language.

The traditional texts, compared to the familiar texts, however, elicited more language from mothers. This may have been due to the fact that more maternal language was needed to support children's participation in this, the more difficult of the two formats. The mothers' job with the traditional, unfamiliar texts may have been to negotiate

Table 3.10 Maternal utterances as targets around traditional texts

Child: antecedent	Mother: target	Child: consequences
	Asks label	
Correct superordinate		Correct answer subordinate
Gives label subordinate		Initiates/labels subordinate
Narrativizes		Not relevant (−)
		Repeat (−)
	Asks subordinate	
Acknowledge		Text–world
Correct superordinate		Describes subordinate
Initiates label superordinate		Not relevant (−)
Not relevant (−)		Incorrect responses
	Expands	
Asks question		Acknowledge
Describes subordinate		Asks question
Initiates/labels subordinate		Expands/extends
Initiates/labels superordinate		Initiates/labels subordinate
Not relevant (−)		Narrativizes
World–text		Not relevant (−)
	Text–world	
Don't know		Acknowledge
World–text		Not relevant (−)
		Text–world
		World–text

Table 3.11 Maternal utterances as targets around familiar texts

Child: antecedent	Mother: target	Child: consequences
	Asks label	
		Correct answer subordinate
		Initiates/labels subordinate
	Asks subordinate	
Correct superordinate		Describes subordinate
'Don't know'		Initiates/labels subordinate
Repeat		Not relevant (−)
	Expands	
Correct superordinate		'Don't know'
Describes subordinate		Initiates/labels subordinate
Not relevant (−)		Not relevant (−)
Text–world	*Text–world*	
		Acknowledge
		Correct answer subordinate
		World–text

Table 3.12 Child utterances as targets around traditional texts

Mother: antecedent	Child: target	Mother: consequence
	Incorrect	
Wh- question		Answers own questions
Asks subordinate		Gives subordinate label
		Negative reinforcement
	Correct answer subordinate	
Answers own questions (–)		Gives superordinate label
Clarify		Reinforce/repeat
Slot/frame		Slot/frame
		Wh-question
	Text–world	
Asks subordinate		Gives label subordinate
Gives label		Reinforce/repeat
Text–world		Wh-question
	World–text	
Linguistic		Expands
World–text		Reinforce/repeat
		Slot/frame
		Text–world
	Initiates superordinate	
		Description
		Slot/frame

meaning for themselves and for the children. This negotiation may have been responsible for the higher frequency.

The familiar format texts did elicit more maternal use of linguistic terms and text–world and world–text utterances. This familiar format may have supported mothers' use of these more sophisticated strategies. Maternal use of linguistic terms was, in turn, significantly correlated with children's use of linguistic terms ($r = 0.90$, $p < 0.0001$). Children's use of linguistic terms was also significantly correlated with maternal expansions ($r = 0.72$, $p < 0.0001$), asking children Wh-questions ($r = 0.60$, $p < 0.01$).

When we look at the sequential lag analyses we find that mothers' use of linguistic terms preceded children's use of linguistic terms at a beyond chance level. It was also the case, however, that when children used linguistic terms, mothers then used them again. It is probably the case that mothers present linguistic terms in the context of asking children questions, children respond using a linguistic term, and mothers reinforce that use by repeating it.

Next we examine the interactions around familiar and traditional texts which relate to vocabulary development. Correlation coefficients between maternal and child utterances generated around traditional and familiar texts and children's vocabulary scores from the PPVT and words taken from the texts are presented in Table 3.9.

First, we considered children's vocabulary as assessed by the PPVT. All of the child utterances and most of the maternal utterances which related to the PPVT were observed around the traditional, not the familiar, texts. The maternal utterances which related to PPVT were: expansions, text–world, world–text, linguistic terms and asks for labels. Children's use of text–world, world–text and linguistic terms, as well as correct answers, was related to their PPVT scores.

The lack of a single significant correlation between children's language observed around familiar text and PPVT scores was surprising. We expected this format to afford children the opportunity to use cognitively and linguistically sophisticated strategies. This was clearly not the case. The obvious question becomes: Why?

The first explanation might be due to a ceiling effect on the familiar setting word lists. This was not the case as the mean score on the familiar lists was 4.95 out of a possible 10. Our preferred explanation relates to the similarities in the design features of the traditional texts and the PPVT. We suggest that both PPVT and traditional texts are 'decontextualized'. In both cases meaning is conveyed via verbal explication, not through shared knowledge or gestures. The higher frequency of talk around the traditional texts is consistent with this argument. Similarly answering questions on the PPVT involved children verbalizing answers. Children's interactions around the traditional texts may have enabled them to address similar demands posed by the PPVT.

Next we addressed more specifically the maternal utterance which related to children's vocabulary. Like the child data, maternal utterances around traditional texts, more than around familiar, related to children's vocabulary. Maternal expansions of children's language, however, were related in both settings. Consistent with past research, expansions are a powerful predictor of child language (Cazden, 1965; Cornell et al., 1988; Dickinson and Smith, 1994).

Lastly, we examined those maternal and child utterances which predicted vocabulary scores. This was done by constructing a matrix of sequential probabilities which preceded and succeeded those utterances. Next, we identified those antecedents and consequential utterances which bound the focal strategies. The sequences for familiar and traditional texts are presented in Tables 3.11 and 3.12, respectively. These results demonstrate the coordination between children and mothers around joint reading. It also demonstrates quite clearly the ways in which mothers maximize children's participation in text-related discourse; this is more commonly done by asking children questions and by expanding upon children's utterances. The role of expansions, as Cazden (1965) showed in the mid-1960s, is a powerful strategy for facilitiating children's language development.

This strategy brings us closer to a discourse level analysis of teaching strategies which predict children's vocabulary development. We think it is important to identify the sequence of utterances, rather than isolated strategies, which are effective. It is this sequence, not isolated utterances, that children and mothers experience.

Implications/conclusions

Data presented in this chapter suggest that joint reading between parents and children is an important crucible for children's literacy learning. More specifically we saw the ways in which maternal strategies which maximized children's participation in the joint reading task related to children's development of literate language, as well as vocabulary. Of particular interest was our finding that LSES mothers and children used similar strategies as do MC dyads. Parents and children from both MC and LSES backgrounds also seem to be sensitive to text level characteristics, such as literary genre. These findings highlight the culturally bound nature of most experimental contexts and of school literacy events. When experimental procedures are made relevant to the groups under study, their performance is maximized. Thus future research should be theoretically motivated in choosing texts around which dyads interact.

Future studies of children's learning literate language in joint reading contexts should be longitudinal. The current work, while consistent with the theory that children internalize maternal dialogue strategies, might also be interpreted as mothers' responding to children's use of linguistic terms. Only a longitudinal design can sort out these antecedent–consequence details.

As we proceed along our developmental path, we now consider the ways in which children use the literate language learned in joint reading in peer contexts.

Chapter 4

Peer interaction, play, and literate language

Naturalistic and experimental evidence from preschool and primary school classrooms

In this chapter we explore some of the ways in which the literate language children are exposed to during joint reading is extended to peer interaction, and eventually into formal school-based literacy events. This discussion extends that of Chapter 3 wherein we noted that children were systematically exposed to literate language in the course of mother–child reading. Thus, one developmental path that we propose is that children are systematically exposed to and taught literate language in the context of joint reading. Children then take these forms and practice using them in pretend play with their peers. After practicing these forms in play children then use them in school-based literacy events. While we do specify developmental pathways, we also note, as we have throughout this work, that there are numerous routes to any developmental outcome, literacy included.

A basic premise of this chapter is that play with peers provides children with opportunities to practice skills and concepts for which they have basic knowledge. Because of the central role of play in our model, we will first define it. Next, we consider the developmental functions of children's play generally, and more specifically in terms of literate behavior. Then, we discuss the two theories of play as practice: Piaget and Vygotsky. Lastly, we examine the ways in which classroom ecological variables, such as play centers and social groupings in those centers, influence children's play and literate language.

Children's play

What is play?

Observers typically state that they can reliably recognize play when they see it but have a difficult time defining it operationally. Given the complexity of the construct, most definitions proffered are multidimensional (Martin and Caro, 1985; Rubin *et al.*, 1983). Rubin and colleagues (1983), for example, define play according to three dimensions: play as psychological disposition, behavior, and contexts supporting play. Animal ethologists also advocate defining play along a number of dimensions (Martin and Caro, 1985), suggesting structural (or behavioral) and consequential (those behaviors following play) criteria.

Probably the most commonly agreed upon definitional criterion for play for both animal and child play scholars is that it does not serve an *immediate* purpose. Rubin *et al.*'s (1983) scheme incorporates purposelessness in its 'means over ends' dispositional criterion. Attending to means rather than ends assumes that children are more concerned with the process of the activity *per se*, than with any outcome of the activity. So, while engaging in block play, children would be concerned with the process of piling and balancing blocks, rather than with the finished project. That the themes of such block building episodes change continuously can be taken as evidence for a means over ends orientation. As we will discuss later in this section, the notion that play is purposeless presents a logical conundrum for scholars who suggest that it serves some developmental function.

The consensus theoretical importance given to the purposelessness criterion does not, however, have quite the same support at the empirical level. In a study of the dispositional criteria of preschool children's play, Smith and Vollstedt (1985) found that nonliterality (or pretense/fantasy), positive affect (or smiling face) and flexibility (or variation in form and context) were the criteria most reliably associated with adults' rating of children's play. Means/ends distinctions did not add to the predictive value in defining play. Of course there is the possibility that adults' perceptions of the criterion are different from children's. Also, the lack of importance in the means/ends distinction for defining play may have been a methodological artifact to the extent that it is a very difficult criterion to observe. Further, the Smith and Vollstedt (1985) study, while a very important and needed first step in defining play, was only one study and we certainly need more research in this area before we dismiss the importance of the means over ends criterion.

In addition to dispositional criteria, play has also been defined according to phenomena which precede and succeed the play behaviors themselves. Rubin *et al.* (1983) defined antecedent conditions to play in terms of 'context', or those situations which support or elicit

play. These contextual or antecedent factors include: a familiar atmosphere (in terms of materials and people), safe and friendly environment, minimally intrusive adults, and children being free from hunger,
stress and fatigue. Animal ethologists use similar criteria in their use
of spatial relations to categorize behavior (Martin and Bateson, 1993).
According to this logic behaviors belong to the same category if they
co-occur in the same context. So, behavior observed in the playground
or in the housekeeping corner of a classroom might be considered play.

Lastly, play can be defined in terms of its consequences. This
approach to defining behavior, which is also labeled motivational or
functional analysis, is typically used by ethologists (e.g. Hinde, 1980)
to infer the meaning of behavior. Meaning for behavior 1 can be
inferred from the consequence it has in behavior 2. A similar approach
has been used in the child developmental literature to define children's
rough-and-tumble play (R and T) by Pellegrini (1988) and define parallel play by Bakeman and Brownlee (1980). For example, children's
fighting behaviors were considered playful (R and T) if games followed R and T; if aggression followed then it was considered aggressive behavior.

While it is useful to use a multidimensional approach to defining
play, it is also important to keep components conceptually distinct,
especially when considering the developmental function of play.

Functions of children's play

As we have noted above, most definitions of play include a statement
that play is purposeless. Yet, and perhaps paradoxically, play is often
conceptualized as serving an important function in the development of
children. From at least the time of Groos (1898, 1901) play has been
considered practice for adulthood. Accordingly, during the period of
extended childhood, children engage in play to learn and practice those
skills important to functioning members of society.

The paradox of purposelessness and function can be resolved by
invoking the notion of deferred benefits. That is, play is purposeless
(and correspondingly costly in terms of expending resources such as
time and energy) during childhood; functions (or corresponding benefits) from the play are deferred until adulthood (Martin and Caro,
1985).

What is it we mean by function? In its most 'ultimate sense' function can be defined in terms of biological adaptation of a species. A
behavior is functional in this ultimate sense (Hinde, 1980) if it adds to

the survival or reproductive success of individuals (genes) over many succeeding generations. Thus the play behaviors that we observe today probably reflect an adaptation to our hunter-gatherer past, rather than to current circumstances (Boulton and Smith, 1992; Symons, 1978). More thorough discussions of the ultimate function of play can be found in Fagen (1981), Hinde (1980), Martin and Caro (1985) and Tinbergen (1963).

Function can also be defined in terms of beneficial consequences during the lifetime of a particular individual. Benefits may be accrued immediately during the period of childhood or deferred until adulthood. For example, social symbolic play during the preschool period may have immediate value in terms of affiliation with a particular peer group or have deferred benefits and relate to subsequent language production skills. It is this notion of function, in terms of beneficial consequence, which most child developmentalists use. Indeed, Vygotsky (1978) explicitly posited that a developmental function of young children's symbolic play was later (deferred) facility with written language.

In this chapter we will discuss beneficial consequences in terms of both immediate and deferred benefits. To the extent that social symbolic play seems most relevant to the development of literacy, this form of play occurs most frequently during the preschool period (Fein, 1981) and that it accounts for a significant portion of children's behavior during this period (Smith and Dodsworth, 1978), we would expect benefits to occur during (immediate benefits) or after this period. Correspondingly, there should be an association between the cost of play (possibly in terms of time spent in this form of play) and benefits.

Generally, the child development literature has not attended to issues of immediate or deferred benefits (notable exceptions include Smith, 1982; Waters and Sroufe, 1983). Most theories of play, from Groos (1898, 1901) through Piaget (1962) and Vygotsky (1978), have proposed that benefits of play are deferred.This assumption may be related to the longstanding developmental bias of the importance of early experience for later development (Bateson, 1981; Gomendio, 1988) and to assumptions of continuity from childhood through adulthood (Kagan, 1983). The purpose of play, a quintessentially child behavior, is typically understood in terms of adult benefits. Bateson (1976) labels this view of play as a 'scaffolding metaphor': play functions in the assembly of skills and then is disassembled when the skill is complete.

With regard to symbolic play, it might aid in the assembly of other representational skills, such as reading and oral language skills, and then disappear. There is not strong empirical support for this claim in either the animal or human play literature (Bekoff and Byers, 1981; Fagen, 1981; Martin and Caro, 1985; Smith, 1982). Despite this state, however, the dominant theories and extant research programs in children's play assume play has deferred benefits.

An alternative, and certainly less common, view of play is that it is not an incomplete or inferior version of some adult behavior but that it is beneficial in its own regard during childhood. In this model, play is metamorphic and has benefits immediate to childhood, and any deferred benefits are not directly apparent or are seen in terms of transformations (Bateson, 1976; Bjorklund and Green, 1992; Gomendio, 1988). The notion that play has immediate benefits grows out of the assumption that it would be a useful and specific adaptation to the niche of childhood. For example, the sense of mastery and self-efficacy associated with children's play may relate to children's experimenting with new and different processes and material. The repetition and variation often associated with play are probably important for learning such things as fine motor skills.

While research in children's play has not examined the immediate benefit hypothesis, animal play researchers have done so extensively. Most notably, Caro's work (Caro, 1982, 1988, 1995; Martin and Caro, 1985) on cats' play proposes that the relatively low costs associated with play (costs in these cases are expressed in terms of caloric expenditure) translate into immediate benefits.

Clearly more work is needed in this area. But how would one go about examining immediate and deferred benefits of play? Here animal ethologists have much to teach us. Most relevant to our discussion are the methods of experimental enhancement or deprivation and design feature arguments.

Design feature arguments

Design feature arguments involve explication of similarities and differences between aspects of play and similar features in mature behavior. Besides being used by animal ethologists, design feature arguments are also used by ethnographers of schooling, such as Heath (1983). Take, for example, one aspect of the language of social symbolic play, the use of explicit oral language. The design features of this form of oral language (e.g. endophora, narrative structure and linguistic terms) are also the design features of school-based literacy lessons. Thus, using this sort of language in play provides opportunities to practice and expand one's facility with these features; this facility, in turn, should predict early school-based literacy.

There are clearly some pitfalls associated with design feature arguments. Any one play behavior, for instance, might serve any one of a number of different functions, only one of which might resemble the original design feature. This is a classic case of discontinuity in development (Kagan, 1971). Similarly, any one mature behavior might have developed via one of many different courses. This is the problem of 'equifinality' in development.

Enhancement/deprivation

Design features can also be experimentally manipulated in either play enhancement or play deprivation experiments. With enrichment experiments, children are given additional opportunities to engage in and/or tuition in specified aspects of play, such as symbolic transformations or reciprocal role taking (e.g. Burns and Brainerd, 1979). Enhancement should result in improved performance on mature skills or concepts of which of these design features are constitutive, e.g. writing and perspective taking. Because of the typically close temporal proximity between enrichment and measurement of outcome measures, most of this research *assumes* that benefits are immediate, not deferred. This point is interesting both because the dichotomy between immediate and deferred benefits is not usually addressed and because of the fact that their stated theoretical orientations (often Piaget or Vygotsky) explicitly propose deferred benefits!

Few deprivation studies have been conducted. Where they have been conducted they have been in the area of physically vigorous play (Pellegrini and Davis, 1993; Pellegrini *et al.*, 1995c; Smith and Hagan, 1980), not forms of play, such as symbolic play, relevant to early literacy, though there may be some 'natural' deprivation experiments to observe. It is probably the case that a number of preschools and kindergarten classrooms 'deprive' children of opportunities to play as they maximize time spent on 'academic' tasks.

The assumption behind deprivation studies, briefly, is that if an aspect of play is important in a certain developmental epoch, then depriving children of the opportunity to engage in that behavior should result in a 'rebound' when children are again given opportunity to play. In short, children overcompensate for the time they have lost during deprivation. It would be interesting to observe the extent to which children experiencing different preschool curricula (i.e. play enriched and play deprived) 'rebound' after school. If symbolic play is important for young children it would be expected that children deprived of play experiences in schools (other things being equal) would engage in symbolic play for longer durations than children experiencing play-enriched curriculum.

With these ideas in mind, we specifically address theories whose thrusts are directly germane to play and early literacy: those of Vygotsky and Piaget.

Vygotsky's and Piaget's theories of play

Vygotsky's theory

Vygotsky (1978) presented play as serving an important developmental function for preschool children. Like Piaget, Vygotsky examined the role of symbolic play during the preschool period and its relation to subsequent mental functioning. Specifically, Vygotsky stated that children's play was governed by two opposing forces. It is catharsis-like (Fein, 1979) where children play to obtain what is not obtainable in reality. For example, children might play at being superstars while they are playing basketball alone. This sort of wish fulfilling behavior should result in children being highly motivated to engage in play. At this level children are motivated to play because they are obtaining the unobtainable.

At another level, however, children try to govern their play according to the societal rules for the behaviors being enacted. For the example given above, it would be important for the child to get the basketball in the hoop. Thus, in their play children are also coming to terms with meeting the demands of societal defined rules and regulations.

The confluence of these two factors (wish fulfilling and rule governed behavior) means that in play children exhibit levels of competence that are not ordinarily observed in more realistic settings. For this reason Vygotsky considered children's play as an example of a zone of proximal development. By this he meant that in play children were able to achieve at higher levels of competence than in reality. It was in the area of symbolic development that Vygotsky most thoroughly discussed play.

It was through symbolic play that Vygotsky believed that children learned to manipulate abstract and socially mediated symbols. Children's play initially relies on realistic props and then becomes less constrained. Through this process children learn the arbitrary relation between signifier and signified. Signifiers, with development, not only become more abstract but also become more similar to socially defined signifiers.

The paradigm case of this developmental process for Vygotsky was in children's learning to write. Using symbols begins with gestures and symbolic play, progresses through drawing and scribbling, and finishes with children's use of standardized orthography in writing. Thus, the level of abstraction here moves from rather idiosyncratic and direct representation (in the case of symbolic play rooted in individualized scenarios enacted with concrete play props). With development the representation moves from first order symbolization (e.g. a picture representing a tree) to second order symbolization (e.g. the written word *tree* representing the oral word *tree*). Engagement in symbolic play for the Vygotskian preschooler, then, should predict children's ability to manipulate other socially defined symbol systems, like alphabetic literacy systems.

Piaget's theory

For Piaget (1962) children's play, generally, was the form taken during childhood of the dominance of assimilation over accommodation. In this sense play had minimal effects on the reorganization of cognitive schemata. Play was a way in which children could subordinate the world to their conceptualizations with minimal change in cognitive structures.

Different 'stages' of cognitive development, for Piaget, were characterized by different types of play. Specifically, the sensorimotor stage was characterized by functional play where infants and toddlers detached functional motor patterns, such as holding and releasing a block, from their ordinary contexts, such as repeatedly dropping the block. The preoperational stage is typified by symbolic play, or activities where a child has one thing representing another. Symbolic representations first are based on object representations (object transformations), such as a doll representing a real baby, and then, later, conducted without the support of objects (i.e. ideational transformations), such as a child proclaiming, 'I'll be the Daddy.'

Importantly, children's symbolic play is rule governed, though the rules are typically established during particular play bouts and undergo continuous renegotiation and change. Thus, symbolic play follows rules, but the rules are idiosyncratic.

During the formal operational period, children's play involves games-with-rules, where behavior is governed by a set of *a priori* rules, such as chess or football. The rules exist, independent of the players involved, thus, children must be able to subordinate their behavior to these rules. In this way, games with rules are very different from other forms of play, such as social symbolic play. Functional and symbolic play is assimilative as children subordinate reality to their conceptualizations, not vice versa, as in games with rules, which are accommodative.

Piaget's scheme for categorizing children's play was taken by the influential Israeli psychologist, Sara Smilansky (1967), and expanded to include 'constructive play'. Her often used system to categorize play included functional, constructive, and dramatic (for symbolic) play, and games. As noted by Smith and colleagues (1986), construction was not considered to be a form of play by other theorists, Piaget included, because it did not meet the all important criterion of being assimilative. Nor did it, as Smith (1988) pointed out, meet the developmental criterion. Specifically, constructive activities are primarily accommodative as children are concerned with end products, not means or processes. Further, the frequency of occurrence of construction does not vary significantly across the preschool period, thus it does not follow the typical inverted-U developmental curve of play.

Our reason for going into this level of detail is that the Smilansky scheme of play was taken by Rubin and colleagues (see Rubin *et al.*, 1983 for a compilation of this work) and conjoined with Parten's (1932) social participation continuum, to form a very influential matrix for categorizing children's play. In a subsequent section of this chapter we will discuss this matrix and its relevance for children's literate language in greater detail.

Role of symbolic play in development

While Piagetian and Vygotskian theory both stressed the role of symbolic play in subsequent cognitive development, the theories are at odds regarding the role of symbolic play in leading, rather than following, developmental changes. We propose that there are elements in each theory which suggest that symbolic play might serve a leading role in cognitive development generally, and in literacy learning specifically.

The basic psychological process motivating developmental change can be reasonably captured with Piaget's equilibration theory. Developmental change, according to this theory, is motivated by conceptual conflict, or disequilibration. Children and adults alike work to re-establish equilibration through assimilation and accommodation; the resulting state is cognitive growth.

Applied to symbolic play, we believe that social symbolic play is more likely to present opportunities for conceptual conflict than solitary symbolic play (Rubin, 1980). When children engage in social symbolic play with peers, they are interacting around themes that are both societally grounded as well as abstract. For example, when children play some superhero episode, the rough outline for their play is derived from an existing societal script. In symbolic play, however, children do not merely reproduce these scripts, they change them in some very idiosyncratic and creative ways. Further, they often use gestures and language which might be ambiguous in the conveyance of meaning.

Both of these factors, the existence of a social script and the existence of ambiguity, as well as the relatively egalitarian nature of peer relations, probably facilitate conceptual conflict. Resolution is likely to occur because of the motivational aspect of social symbolic play: children enjoy the activity so they do what they can to maintain it. Thus in order to understand the developmental significance of children's play it is crucial to describe both social and cognitive dimensions of play.

Social and cognitive dimensions of children's play.

In the mid-1970s a leading play researcher, Kenneth H. Rubin (Rubin *et al.*, 1976; Rubin *et al.*, 1978), illustrated very nicely the importance of considering both social and cognitive dimensions of children's play. Cognitive aspects of play were represented by Smilansky's four levels of play (functional, constructive, dramatic and games) and social participation was judged in terms of an adaptation of Parten's (1932) classic paper (solitary, parallel and interactive behavior). The two systems

	Functional	Constructive	Dramatic	Games
Solitary				
Parallel				
Interactive				

Figure 4.1 Smilansky–Parten matrix

were combined into a matrix (as represented in Figure 4.1) so that social and cognitive dimensions of behavior could be considered simultaneously.

This matrix has been most typically used by considering the variation in each of the twelve categories due to such factors as age, gender and classroom context (see Rubin et al., 1983 for a summary of this work). Researchers have also conducted extensive research into the social and cognitive implications of these categories.

Most typically, studies have been conducted whereby correlations between each of the twelve categories was correlated with some outcome measure. So, for example, solitary functional play is negatively and significantly correlated with rating of hyperactivity–distractibility by preschool supervisors (Rubin and Clarke, 1982).

The original twelve categories were reduced in subsequent studies for a number of reasons. First, many of the twelve measures are intercorrelated so analysis of individual categories resulted in Type 1 error. In one factor analytical study, Pellegrini (1986) found that the twelve categories reduced to three factors: dramatic-constructive play, functional-constructive play and solitary behavior. Age for preschool children loaded negatively on solitary behavior. Additionally, in light of the fact that most studies centered on preschool-age children, the games-with-rules category was omitted simply because children of this age do not exhibit this behavior with any frequency (Pellegrini, 1980); thus many studies utilized nine categories.

Naturalistic studies of children in preschool classrooms reliably showed that the nature of their behavior followed the themes inherent in the props. Children were more likely to engage in constructive activity with art materials and blocks than with housekeeping props (Pellegrini, 1984b; Pellegrini and Perlmutter, 1989). Further, social-contextual variables also related to play. Adult presence tended to inhibit children's dramatic play (Pellegrini, 1984b) and their use of imaginative language (Pellegrini, 1983). Also when children were together, compared to alone, with blocks, their play was frequently dramatic (Rubin et al., 1983; Pellegrini, 1984b).

The gist of these studies using the Smilansky–Parten matrix, then, is that children's fantasy is elicited by housekeeping props and inhibited by adult presence. By the time children are 3-years-of-age they are quite capable of sustained peer play. All they seem to need is a supportive context of play props and minimal adult intrusion. We now describe more exactly the extent to which these play contexts elicit literate language.

Uses of literate language in preschool play contexts

In this section we examine in closer detail the ways in which children's use of literate language is supported or inhibited in preschool class-rooms. Our initial examinations of the role of play, literate language and early literacy were motivated by rather global studies of play where we found correlations between the frequency with which children engaged in symbolic play and early reading ability (Pellegrini, 1980).

Study 1: an initial examination of uses of literate language while playing

We examined the actual language that children used when interacting with pretend play props and with constructive play props (Pellegrini, 1982). In this naturalistic study, we observed four young children as they played in their preschool classroom. Our initial conceptualizations of symbolic play and literate language was guided by the work of both M. A. K. Halliday and David Olson. As noted earlier Olson's (1977) notion of literacy was one where meaning was verbally expli-cated, not assumed. This form of language resembled Bernstein's (1960) descriptions of elaborated language.

Correspondingly, Halliday (1969–70), in discussions of functions of language, noted that when using the 'imaginative function' of language children had to make meaning verbally explicit in order for it to be understood by other players. The ambiguity and fantastic nature of pre-tend play meant, according to Halliday, that speakers could only min-imally rely upon gestures and shared knowledge to convey meaning. A stick in a pretend play episode took on a different meaning, a mean-ing that had to be explicitly defined if other players were to understand its new role.

Halliday's description of the register used to serve the imaginative function of language, like Olson's description of literate language, stressed explicated meaning. We thought that a particularly important dimension of this register was children's use of cohesive oral language (Halliday and Hasan, 1976).

At a global level, cohesion was defined by Halliday and Hasan as the extent to which meaning was established within a text by a series of interconnected ties. So, for example, a child playing might say the following:

1 This stick is my gun.

Here the word **this** is made meaningful within the text by its tie to **stick**. This sort of endophoric tie is a paradigm example of literate langauge, where meaning is carried by text, not context.

Meaning can also be carried by context, through the use of exophora, as in the next example.

> 2 This is my gun.

In this case the child defines the **gun** contextually, by holding up the stick. In order for the word **this** to be understood unambiguously in utterance 2, speaker and listener must be able to see each other. This sort of text is not cohesive because the meaning is not derived from intertextual ties. As we know, literacy events often involve physical, as well as psychological, distance between writer and reader, thus reliance on exophoric reference is not a characteristic of literate language.

Method

In our study, four preschool children (two girls and two boys, age 51–60-months) were observed playing in their classroom with dramatic play props (e.g. dress-up clothes and play sink, stove, telephone and refrigerator) and blocks (Pellegrini, 1982). Children were videotaped in each of these settings for 30 minutes. Utterances were then transcribed according to Halliday and Hasan's model of cohesion.

Results/discussion

We observed a total of ten constructive and pretend play episodes. Generally, the pretend episodes were more explicit than were the constructive. In the pretend episodes, players introduced play themes explicitly, often in response to listeners' needs for clarification. For example:

> 3 *S1*:   The red one. I want the red one.
> *S2*:   The red one?
> *S1*:   The red hat. There's only one over there.

In this case, S1 introduces a new topic with **The red one**, but S2 doesn't know what the red one is and asks for clarification by repeating the introductory utterance with a questioning intonation. The initiator then clarifies one with an endophoric tie: **one** is tied to **hat**.

This investigation also pointed to the importance of explicit topic introductions. The roles and definitions presented in the introductions and their ensuing clarifications were the bases for subsequent cohesive ties. That is, after roles and definitions were initially established, children tied subsequent utterances to them, through a variety of means, such as pronominal and demonstrative reference. The importance of endophoric reference for sustained pretend play was supported by the finding that only 9 percent of the references were exophoric in pretend play episodes compared with 21 percent in constructive activities.

While these results were interesting and supportive of our hypotheses we wanted to replicate and extend them. Specifically we wanted to experimentally manipulate children's exposure to dramatic and constructive play themes. This would allow us to make a clearer statement about the role of dramatic play on literate language. We also wanted to extend our notions of literate beyond cohesive ties, to include other dimensions of literate language as described by both Halliday and Olson.

Study 2: an experimental study of the effect of props on preschool children's literate language

In this study (Pellegrini, 1985, 1986) we present the effects of preschool children interacting in experimental dramatic and constructive settings. We were interested in replicating the results of Study 1 where the dramatic, compared to the constructive, setting was associated with more cohesive language. The experimental manipulation would allow us to rule out differences due to self-selection factors.

Also interesting was a further exploration of dimensions of literate language. In Study 1 we examined only cohesive ties as a measure of literate language. In this study we included not only endophoric and exophoric reference, but also children's use of 'meta' talk, or language about linguistic and cognitive processes. Following Olson's (1977) theory, becoming literate involves being able to reflect upon the linguistic processes associated with making meaning explicit. Olson and colleagues (Torrance and Olson, 1984) have demonstrated that talk about these processes does predict school-based literacy.

We knew from Bernstein and Halliday that explicitness could be measured by the children's use of modifiers and qualifiers around pronouns, or heads. Simply, use of modifiers which immediately precede a noun or pronoun, and qualifiers which immediately follow, verbally elaborates the noun. Take the following two examples:

4   [The big red] house {down the street} is mine.
5   [The big] house is mine.

In cases 4 and 5, respectively, we see three and two words as modifiers, bounded by [ ], and three words as qualifiers, bounded by { }. The 'verbal picture' in case 4 is much more vivid than that in case 5. Thus the advantage of using modifiers and qualifiers, in conjunction with endophoric reference, as a measure of verbal explicitness.

Lastly we were concerned with the 'narrative organization' of children's language in both play settings. Narrative structure of language was important, we thought, because narratives are the primary genre of school-based literacy events (Galda *et al.*, 1996). That is, when children are taught to read, they typically read 'stories', or narratives. Similarly, when they are asked to write in school, stories are expected.

Some scholars, most notably Denny Wolf (Wolf and Grollman, 1982), Shirley Brice Heath (1982) and Lee Galda (1984), have pointed to similarities between narrative and pretend play. Both involve the suspension of reality, telling stories (often characterized by the use of temporal and causal conjunctions, as well as past tense verbs) and enactment of fictional roles (Galda, 1984; Heath, 1982). For that reason we examine the occurrences of narrative structure in these two play settings.

Narrative structure of children's play was defined here, following Wolf and Grollman (1982), according to the degree of sequential elaboration on a single pretend theme. A one utterance theme, such as holding a spoon to a doll's mouth and saying 'Open', was coded as a scheme. Two or three goal oriented schemes, such as saying 'Open', then dipping the spoon into pretend cereal, and offering it to the doll, were considered simple events; contoured events had at least four different schemes, such as pouring milk into cereal, adding sugar, dipping spoon into bowl and feeding doll.

More complex were episodes. Simple episodes contained two or more simple events; for example, taking the simple event described above, the speaker adds the following: taking off doll's nappy, washing it, adding powder, and a new nappy. Contoured episodes are two or more contoured events.

We expected, of course, that the dramatic setting, compared to the constructive setting, would elicit more literate language. We also expected that children would utilize more literate language as a function of age. For this reason we observed children from two age groups, 4- and 5-years-of-age.

Method

Twenty children (ten girls and ten boys, half of whom were 4- and the other half 5-years-of-age) participated in this study. They all attended the University of Georgia (UGA) preschool and were predominantly middle class children.

An observer with whom the children were familiar (she had spent the preceding two weeks in their classroom playing with them) escorted them to an experimental playroom in their school. She then left the room and went into an adjacent room and videotaped them through a one-way viewing mirror. The playroom was also equipped with microphones suspended from the ceiling so that sound could be recorded. Children were observed in same gender, same age dyads in the playroom, in two 20-minute sessions with dramatic props and on two occasions with constructive props. The social configurations were based on teachers' nomination of children who usually played together. Props in each setting were similar to those found in the classrooms.

The dramatic props were as follows: two doctors' kits, two smocks, blankets and pill bottles. The constructive props included: wooden and colorful blocks of various sizes, numerous Styrofoam shapes (taken from stereo packing boxes) and pipe cleaners.

Children's language and corresponding actions from all observations were transcribed verbatim and coded according to the above noted aspects of literate language.

Results/discussion

Descriptive statistics for literate language, by age and play context, are displayed in Table 4.1. Table 4.2 displays the intercorrelations among the separate dimensions of literate language. Results from this study confirm those reported in Study 1. Generally, children produced more literate language in dramatic than in constructive settings

While more endophora and modifiers and qualifiers were observed in the dramatic setting, compared to the constructive, the differences were not statistically significant, probably due to the small sample size. In this study the dyad, not the individual, was the unit of analysis. We did, however, observe a statistically significant difference in the expected direction for exophora, with more being observed with block than with dramatic props. Thus, there is a tendency for children to be more verbally explicit in dramatic play than in constructive play.

The dramatic setting also elicited significantly more linguistic verbs

Table 4.1 Means (M)* and standard deviations (SD) for linguistic measures by age, by context

| | Verbs | | Linguistic | | Cognitive | | Nominal | | | | | |
| | Words | | | | | | Modifier | | Head | | Qualifier | |
Centers	M	SD	M	SD	M	SD	M	SD	M	SD	M	SD
Blocks	529.65	227.23	0.008	0.006	0.01	0.009	0.24	0.04	0.36	0.03	0.50	0.16
4 years	586.90	185.73	0.006	0.003	0.01	0.009	0.23	0.05	0.35	0.03	0.50	0.19
5 years	472.40	268.73	0.01	0.01	0.02	0.01	0.25	0.04	0.37	0.04	0.51	0.13
Housekeeping	622.65	316.33	0.009	0.007	0.02	0.009	0.31	0.06	0.34	0.02	0.52	0.12
4 years	526.30	235.80	0.008	0.006	0.03	0.01	0.22	0.06	0.35	0.02	0.52	0.16
5 years	719.00	396.86	0.01	0.009	0.02	0.009	0.29	0.06	0.33	0.03	0.53	0.09

| | Pronouns | | | | | | Reference | | | | Tense | | | | | | | |
| | 1st | | 2nd | | 3rd | | Exophora | | Endophora | | Present | | Past | | Future | | Non-present | |
	M	SD	M	SD	M	SD	M	SD	M	SD	M	SD	M	SD	M	SD	M	SD
Blocks	0.09	0.04	0.06	0.03	0.12	0.02	0.18	0.05	0.12	0.03	0.12	0.02	0.01	0.005	0.04	0.01	0.19	0.04
4 years	0.09	0.03	0.06	0.02	0.09	0.03	0.18	0.06	0.12	0.04	0.13	0.03	0.01	0.001	0.04	0.01	0.16	0.03
5 years	0.09	0.05	0.07	0.04	0.16	0.04	0.18	0.07	0.12	0.03	0.11	0.02	0.01	0.01	0.05	0.01	0.23	0.05
Housekeeping	0.07	0.01	0.05	0.01	0.15	0.06	0.16	0.02	0.13	0.06	0.11	0.02	0.01	0.008	0.05	0.01	0.22	0.06
4 years	0.09	0.01	0.06	0.01	0.12	0.06	0.16	0.03	0.13	0.06	0.11	0.02	0.01	0.01	0.05	0.01	0.19	0.07
5 years	0.06	0.01	0.05	0.01	0.18	0.06	0.16	0.02	0.13	0.06	0.11	0.02	0.01	0.006	0.05	0.006	0.25	0.05

Note
* Means for all measures, except words, are proportional to the number of words.

Table 4.2 Significant intercorrelations among dependent variables*

	Mod	Qual	V. cog	V. ling	V. past	V. pres	V. fut	V. past & fut	1st P	2nd P	3rd P
Exo	0.74	0.70	0.66			0.83	0.82	0.82		0.79	
Endo	0.79	0.75	0.90		0.68	0.89	0.72	0.81	0.68		0.73
Mod		0.84	0.88		0.77	0.91	0.94	0.97	0.64	0.81	0.71
Qual	0.84		0.83	0.68		0.77	0.87	0.85		0.83	0.76
V. cog	0.88	0.83		0.64	0.77	0.85	0.83	0.88			0.71
V. ling		0.68	0.64								0.84
V. past	0.77		0.77			0.77	0.64	0.76	0.69		
V. pres	0.91	0.77	0.85		0.77		0.91	0.94	0.77	0.77	0.67
V. fut	0.94	0.87	0.83		0.64	0.91		0.98	0.64	0.81	
V. past & fut	0.97	0.85	0.88		0.76	0.94	0.98		0.69	0.82	0.65
1stP	0.64				0.69	0.77	0.64	0.69			
2ndP	0.81	0.83				0.77	0.81	0.82			
3rdP	0.71	0.76	0.71	0.84		0.67		0.65			

Notes

Exo = Exophora; Endo = Endophora; Mod = Modifiers; Qual = Qualifiers; V. cog = cognitive verbs; V. ling = linguistic verbs; V. past = past tense verbs; V. pres = present tense verbs; V. fut = future tense verbs; 1stP = 1st person pronouns; 2ndP = 2nd person pronouns; 3rdP = 3rd person pronouns

*df = 8[n(10) − 2], $p<0.05$, $r = 0.63$, $p<0.01$, $r = 0.76$

than the constructive setting. It was probably the case that children used these terms as part of the process by which they clarified meaning. For example, one child, in directing the play episode, said: 'No, I said start now'. In another case a child asked another to 'Say that again' so as to sustain a play episode. Thus the social negotiation inherent in social pretend play, including disagreements and ambiguity, affords children the opportunity to reflect upon the social and linguistic processes constitutive of their interaction.

That older children were facile with many aspects of literate language was supported by the robust age effects on higher levels of narrative production (contoured events and simple and contoured episodes) as well as use of metalanguage and modifiers and qualifiers. The descriptive statistics for these analyses are presented in Table 4.3 and Figure 4.2.

Regarding the narrative structure of children's interaction, minimal main effects for setting were observed. Setting did, however, interact statistically with children's age such that older children (5-year-olds), compared to younger children's (4-year-olds), produced more contoured episodes with the constructive props. These results may indicate that the explicit definition inherent in the dramatic props might have afforded opportunities for children to engage in sustained play.

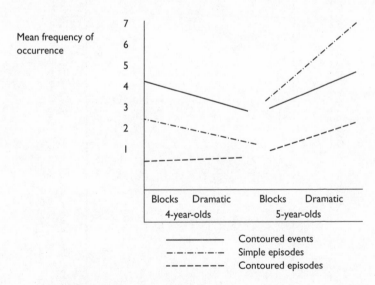

Figure 4.2 Significant main and interactive effects of age and play contexts on the narrative organization of play

Table 4.3 Descriptive statistics* for narrative organization of play by age by play context

	Scheme	Event	Contoured event	Episode	Contoured episode	Variety	Total
4 years	6.60 (4.39)	4.30 (2.73)	3.30 (2.41)	0.08 (0.78)	2.20 (1.43)	4.50 (0.76)	17.20 (7.81)
Blocks	6.20 (4.13)	5.20 (3.29)	3.80 (1.54)	0.08 (0.78)	2.60 (1.83)	4.40 (0.89)	18.60 (7.05)
Dramatic	7.00 (4.66)	3.40 (2.17)	2.80 (3.29)	0.80 (0.78)	1.80 (1.03)	4.60 (0.54)	15.80 (8.58)
5 years	3.90 (2.43)	4.30 (2.44)	3.90 (2.35)	1.90 (1.10)	5.20 (2.58)	4.70 (0.67)	19.20 (7.17)
Blocks	2.60 (1.07)	4.20 (2.61)	3.20 (2.34)	1.80 (1.54)	4.00 (2.30)	4.40 (1.34)	15.80 (6.45)
Dramatic	5.20 (3.79)	4.40 (2.27)	4.60 (2.36)	2.00 (0.66)	6.40 (2.87)	5.00 (0.00)	22.60 (7.89)

Note:
* Standard deviations are in parentheses.

When the props had less clear definition, as with the constructive props, only the older children had the facility to generate a complex narrative line.

When narrative themes were present in play props all children generated rather complex narratives: the structure of the narrative was probably supported by the explicit and common theme of the doctor props. When there was no explicit narrative theme inherent in the props, children had to come up with a theme and communicate to their peers in such a way that it was both understood and interesting. This was clearly a difficult task because it not only necessitated that they present a narrative theme but also required them to use explicit language to redefine the props and their roles in relation to this theme.

The importance of narratives for children, as we have suggested in this chapter, relates to their role in school-based literacy events. Current thinking on the role of narratives in children's lives suggests that they may serve another, more effective role. In this sense narrative language, and narrative thought, are personal and bound closely to the immediate context. Children seem to use narratives as one way in which they understand difficult and sometimes stressful events (Bruner, 1986). When confronted with a challenging situation, children may use some form of personal story as a way of understanding the situation. So in the case of being presented with ambiguous play props young children often use personal narratives as one way in which to establish interactions with peers (Pellegrini and Galda, 1988). It would be interesting to know the degree to which more context free language and thought, or what Bruner (1986) called paradigmatic thought, followed these personal narratives.

In conclusion, results from Study 2 provide support for our hypothesis that literate language is facilitated in pretend play settings. The impact of pretend seems particularly robust for children's metalanguage. We propose that the process of social negotiation inherent in social pretend play is responsible for children's use of 'meta' language. These results beg the obvious question: to what degree do these oral language forms relate to formal school-based literacy? This question is addressed in Study 3.

Study 3: symbolic play predicting early reading and writing

In this investigation we considered the extent to which preschoolers' symbolic play and use of linguistic terms predicted reading and writing status (Pellegrini and Galda, 1991). A longitudinal design allowed us to chart the development of children's use of literate language across time, as well as to make antecedent-consequence inferences about play, oral language and becoming literate across the preschool period.

The developmental nature of our questions necessitated a longitudinal design. As noted earlier, theories of early literacy, most notably Vygotsky's (1978), predict that symbolic play would be a developmental precursor to learning to write and read. Symbolic play, Vygotsky argued, was a form of first order symbolization where playful representations represent an object.

We suggest that the social context of pretend play enables children's symbolization to move from first order to second order. When children talk about their play transformations and talk about talk they are engaging in second order symbolization: using symbols (in this case talk) to reflect upon other symbols (either play transformations or talk about roles and transformations).

For these reasons we observed the nature of children's play transformations as well as the accompanying forms of language. Transformations were coded, following McLoyd (1980), as object transformations (where an object is actually used in the act) or ideational transformations (where there is no object used). Metalanguage, as an indicator of second order symbolization, was also coded, but differently from previous studies. In this study we considered talk about talk, following Shatz et al.'s (1983) work on talk about internal states, as belonging to one of three categories: idiomatic, regular and contrastive. Idiomatic cases, such as 'You can say that again', are not indicative of reflection upon the linguistic process; they are used formulaically, not reflectively. Regular uses of linguistic terms, such as 'Tell me again what you mean', are indicative of some level of reflection. Most reflective are contrastive terms, such as 'You can't say that'.

We followed a sample of children across a two-year span to the end of the preschool period (5-years-of-age), using measures of play transformations and metalanguage at time 1 to predict literacy at time 2.

Method

A sample of twelve children attending the University of Georgia laboratory preschool were observed across the period of two academic years. These mostly middle class children (five girls and seven boys) had a mean age of 43-months at the start of year 1 and 64-months at the end of year 2.

Children were observed in their preschool classrooms monthly for nine months in each of the two years. This was accomplished by having children wear wireless microphones in a vest. Their voices were projected via FM radio signal to a receiver and tape recorder in an observation booth. Children said their names and dates upon putting on the vests. They wore the vests for 15 minutes and their corresponding free play behavior (coded as object or ideational transformations) was coded by an observer in the observation booth.

A number of psychometric measures were also administered to the children. These measures, it should be noted, were not administered by the same persons conducting the observations. In this way we minimized tester and observer bias. At the mid-point of year 1 children took the PPVT. Children's reading and writing status was also measured in the spring of each of the two years.

Children's reading was assessed by two means. First, Clay's (1985) *Concepts about Print* (CAP) was administered. CAP is a reliable and valid measure of children's reading ability and it assesses children's understanding of conventions surrounding literacy teaching. For example, children are handed a standard book to read and they are assessed on such things as whether they hold the book right-side-up and turn pages left-to-right.

Reading was also measured by children's ability to read two children's books which had just been read to them by an experimenter. Their re-readings were coded according to our adaptation of Sulzby's (1987) re-reading 11-point scale (roughly measuring attempts governed by pictures and attempts governed by print). We scored the highest strategies that children exhibited in their re-readings and took the average of the two. This scale is displayed in Table 4.4.

Writing was also assessed twice during the spring of each year. Children wrote about the books they had read and we coded the writing using our adapted system of Sulzby's writing scale. We coded the writing using the high point from the 9-point scale (which goes from drawing to using conventional orthography). Again, we took the average of the two scores. This scale is displayed in Table 4.5.

Results/discussion

We will first discuss children's reading and writing as measured by the CAP and our adaptations of Sulzby's measures. These intercorrelations within each year and across years are displayed in Table 4.6. Children's reading as assessed by both sets of measures was

Table 4.4 Re-reading scale

A *Attempts governed by pictures*

    1 *Labeling*: The child merely labels (rather than describes) individual pictures.

    2 *Action-governed attempts*: The child describes individual pictures without using past tense, temporal markers and endophora.

    3 *Disconnected oral dialogue*: The child does not use exclusively pictures to tell a story. One or many partial stories are given. The child uses past tense and temporal markers.

    4 *Stories told for audience*: The child tells connected stories by pointing to or attending to the pictures, not the print. These stories are characterized by endophora and a temporal ordering of the different pictures into a story – that is, they use the pictures to form a cohesive story.

    5 *Created story*: The child's story uses the same characters as are in the text but a different sequence of events.

    6 *Similar to written text*: The child creates a story that resembles the original but is not a verbatim account.

    7 *Verbatim-like attempts*: The child points to the pictures, not the print, and tells a memorized story.

B *Attempts governed by print*

    8 *Print-governed refusal*: The child refuses to try to read the print because he or she cannot read print.

    9 *Aspectual attempts*: The child focuses on one or more of the following aspects of reading at the expense of the whole:

        (a) Letter/sound (tries to sound out words)

        (b) Known words (reads only known words)

        (c) Comprehension (tries to recite the text from memory)

   10 *Strategy-dependent*: The child reads, but he or she overemphasizes one or more strategies (for example, explicitly sounding out words). Children can use these strategies but they are not used to integrate words or used flexibly.

   11 *Independent readings*: The child is actually reading print.

Table 4.5 Writing scale

---

1 *Drawing*: children drew pictures of the story they were asked to write.

2 *Scribbling*: children used curved lines which did not resemble words.

3 *Letter-like units*: children used graphic signs that resembled letters but were not letters.

4 *Well-learned units*: children repeated the use of individual letters.

5 *Invented spelling*: children used their own spelling where they had a symbol for each phoneme/word.

6 *Conventional orthography*: children used the conventional letter forms and spellings for individual words.

Table 4.6 Partial intercorrelations[a] among literacy measures by year

	Within year 1[b]			Within year 2[b]			Year 1 to 2[b]		
	1	2	3	1	2	3	1	2	3
Concepts about Print (1)		0.27	0.18		0.61**	0.38	0.26	0.24	0.02
Highest writing (2)			0.18			0.25		0.04	0.50*
Highest reading (3)								0.29	0.67*

Notes
[a] PPVT is partialled out
[b] $N = 12$
* $p < 0.10$
** $p < 0.05$

Table 4.7 Significant coefficients between metalinguistic verbs and fantasy transformations by year

	Within year 1				Within year 2		Year 1 to 2				
	1	2	3	4	1	2	1	2	3	4	5
Metaling: idiom (1)	0.54*						0.50*				
Metaling: process (2)		0.68*				0.77**					
Metaling: contrast (3)	0.91***	0.63**			0.50*	0.80***			0.55*		
Object (4)	0.94***	0.62**				0.90***					0.84***
Idea (5)				0.95***							0.83***

Notes
$N = 12$
* $p < 0.10$
** $p < 0.05$
*** $p < 0.01$

intercorrelated significantly as was the relationship between both measures of writing. Thus our use of the 'highest score' on our adaptation of Sulzby's measures of reading and writing was a valid indicator of these constructs.

Next, we consider the use of linguistic terms. All three forms of linguistic verbs tended to co-occur with object and ideational transformations. The intercorrelations among these measures within and across years are displayed in Table 4.7. These findings confirm our earlier claims that fantasy supports this level of reflection upon language.

While each of the three forms of linguistic verbs co-occurred across the two years, only the regular and contrastive terms seem to indicate that children were actually reflecting upon language. Only these two forms predicted children's reading and writing within each of the two years and from year 1 to year 2, even when the PPVT and year 1 reading and writing status were controlled. The regression models for year 1 are presented in Tables 4.8 and 4.9. The partial correlations for year 1 terms predicting literacy in year 2 are presented in Table 4.10. Thus, the importance of talk about talk as a developmental precursor to formal school-based literacy was confirmed. That is, our conceptualization of early literacy as children's talk about talk was confirmed: children's talk about talk predicted ability to read and write on measures of school-based literacy.

Next we examined the relation between modes of play transformation and children's writing. Our analysis strategy, as in the case of reading, was to control year 1 writing status and correlate measures of play. We found, first, that both forms of play were highly intercorrelated. Further both measures of play in year 1 predicted children's year 2 writing status, but only one of the two measures of reading (see Table 4.7).

These findings, interpreted in terms of Vygotsky's notions of first and second order symbolization, suggest that children's play and early writing are both examples of first order symbolizations. Writing for these children may be more like drawing where the signs they use represent objects, not words. Reading and the use of metalanguage, on the other hand, seem to be second order symbolizations where children are using language to talk about language and treat written words as representations of oral words.

Table 4.8 Significant* predictors of children's highest level of reading status by age

Variable	Steps entered		df	B-value	R^2	F
Older						
IQ	Forced	1	1,14	0.006	0.009	0.12
Process meta-verbs		2	2,14	0.07	0.19	2.69
Younger						
IQ	Forced	1	1,13	0.0005	0.01	0.00
Idiomatic meta-verbs		2	2,14	-1.07	0.44	8.77

Note
*p = <0.05

Table 4.9 Significant* predictors of children's highest level of writing status by age

Variable	Steps entered		df	B-value	R^2	F
Older						
IQ	Forced	1	1,14	0.03	0.26	4.65
Play objects trans		2	2,14	0.08	0.43	3.47
Idiomatic meta-verbs		3	3,14	-0.65	0.55	4.56
Younger						
IQ	Forced	1	1,14	0.13	0.25	3.99

Note
*p = <0.05

Table 4.10 Partial[a] correlations for play transformations and metalinguistic verbs predicting literacy

	Year 2: Concepts about print	High reading	High writing
Year 1			
Metalinguistic: idiomatic	0.45	0.23	−0.20
Metalinguistic: process	0.67**	0.61**	0.62**
Metalinguistic: contrast	0.51*	0.65**	0.51*
Transformation			
Object	0.45**	0.39	0.63**
Ideational	0.44*	0.38	0.62**

Notes
N = 12
[a] Partialled-out of the relations are children's PPVT scores and year 1 levels of criterion measures noted for year 2.
* p = <0.10
** p = <0.05

Conclusion

In this chapter we have demonstrated the oral language basis of early literacy. We suggested that the forms of language that children learned in the context of mother–child book reading, most especially talk about talk, would be taken by children and used with their peers in play. This was supported and replicated in all studies presented. We found that this sort of 'meta' talk first appeared in peer fantasy, then in more realistic peer discourse. Consistent with our conceptualization of literate language being a developmental precursor to school-based literacy, talk about talk, in turn, predicted children's status on school-based reading and writing measures. Importantly, we found that there were different levels of talk about talk. Use of idiomatic phrases clearly were not indicative of metalanguage. This is a consideration for future research.

Also a consideration for future research was the remainder of our proposed developmental pathway, from pretend play with peers to use of these terms with peers in literacy events. In the next chapter we examine this segment of the developmental pathway to literacy.

Chapter 5

Social networks at home and school

Diverse social contacts as affordances for literacy development

In the preceding chapters we have been making an argument for the importance of social interaction in children's learning to use literate language. We began with the idea that children were systematically exposed to literate language while being read to by their mothers. Children learned literate language, we suggested, and then used it with peers, first in fantasy interactions and then in realistic discourse. In Chapter 4 we concentrated on young children, preschoolers, interacting with their peers in pretend play. We suggested that it was the *social* dimension of pretend play that fostered the use of literate language. In this chapter and the next, we begin to examine in more depth the specific aspects of the peer context which support literate language, and, eventually, early literacy. A more thorough explication of the meaning of dimensions of social context for early literacy is clearly a timely task.

Explicating social context

That social context is viewed as important in the early literacy research community is an understatement. Guided by the rehabilitated theory of Vygotsky, many researchers in educational and developmental psychology, as well as in other fields of education, consider literacy as a socially constructed phenomenon. The mother–child book reading paradigm, and all the importance assigned to it, is the paradigm case of the social context of literacy development. We know much less, however, about other social configurations and their effects on early literacy.

The two main objectives of this chapter are to explore more exactly the nature of children's social configurations in early literacy learning events. To our knowledge, very little is known about children's social contacts outside of school. First, we will document the social config-urations in both home and school literacy events for a group of first grade children in Athens, GA.

The second, and associated, goal of this chapter is to specify more exactly what is meant by social context. Given the recognized impor-tance of social context, the time is ripe to specify more exactly those aspects of social context which relate to literate language. Of course, this search must be guided by a theory specifying context–language relations.

Theories of social context and language

Theory, especially Vygotskian theory (Wertsch, 1979), specifies that social interaction (in this case between a child and a tutor) should relate to executive cognitive functions, such as the ability to plan, monitor and reflect upon activities. These abilities, especially the abilities to monitor and reflect upon language, are especially important in early literacy development. As Adams (1990) has shown in her thorough and inte-grative review of the early literacy research, children's ability to reflect upon language, or 'metalinguistic awareness', is a, if not *the*, robust predictor of learning to read. Children's ability to talk about language is an indicator of this ability.

We know from Bernstein's theory (1960, 1971) that speakers' abil-ity to reflect upon language (as part of their reflection upon social roles) is maximized when they interact with a variety of social partners and/or take on a variety of social roles. When speakers interact with different sorts of people and take on different roles they are continually faced with the chore of analyzing audience knowledge and adjusting their talk to these different audiences. Reflection upon the sorts of language that get used in different situations is part of this process.

As Bernstein's theory specified, children are socialized at home into taking on roles. In some families children experience numerous roles as they negotiate their status in different situations. For example, the extent to which children do chores and get paid for them may be nego-tiated between children and adults. In other circumstances, roles are assigned, not negotiated; consequently, children have more restricted role experience. For example, children may be told the chores to do and the pay they will receive. The role is not up for negotiation: par-ents assign roles and children comply.

That the ability to negotiate different roles transfers to school is con-sistent with a number of theories besides Bernstein's adaptation of

Durkheimian theory, including social cognitive theory (Bandura, 1986) and Piagetian (1983) theory. Piagetian theory, however, would specify that children's ability to analyze and adjust behavior in varied social arrangements is a reflection of more general cognitive decentration, or perspective-taking, status (or the ability to view events from a variety of perspectives). Thus we might expect the sort of model shown in Figure 5.1.

Empirical evidence: the role of diverse social context

The research reported in this chapter builds upon the early work exploring the continuity/discontinuity between home and school literacy learning. The early British studies, directly motivated by Bernstein's work, of Tizard and Hughes (1984) and Wells (1984) were very instructive in terms of methodology and showing that SES differences in children's home language was minimal. These findings of minimal SES differences are certainly consistent with our joint reading results reported above. The early British studies also established important empirical links between the sorts of language (what we label literate language) used at home and success in school.

While this work was ground breaking we still need information on the specific social arrangements of early literacy events at home. We still need to know with whom children speak, how they speak with different interlocutors, and in different social arrangements relate to literacy. From the work of Anderson and colleagues (1988) we learned that home literacy diaries can provide important information on children's literacy-related habits. Their use of diaries enabled them to indirectly enter children's homes and document children's choice of reading materials as well as the time they spent reading. These factors were, in turn, related to school reading achievement.

In the study reported in this chapter we used diaries, as well as other

Varied social network: home

Perspective taking   Varied social networks: school

Literate language

School-based literacy

Figure 5.1 Perspective taking

measures of the home environment, to specify an important dimension of children's literacy experiences: the variety of social participants in home literacy events. We then gauged home to school continuity using direct observations of children's social networks in their classrooms.

Method

Participants in this study (Pellegrini *et al.*, 1995a) were drawn from two first grade classrooms in Athens, GA. Participation was determined by informed parental consent. The sample consisted of thirty-five mixed SES children (sixteen girls and nineteen boys) with a mean age of 65-months at the beginning of the school year. In one of the classrooms, a teacher (BS) was also a member of our research team.

Classroom observations began on the second day of the school year for the children. All members of the research team met with children and spent time interacting with them. By the second week of class one member of the research team, not including BS, observed in each classroom until the winter holiday break. Thereafter, and until the end of the year, an observer was in each classroom every other week. Two observers alternated between classrooms.

All children were audiotaped in counterbalanced order once per month for the nine months of the study. Observation rules followed focal child sampling, continuous recording rules (Pellegrini, 1996). We aimed to have 20-minute observation periods but this varied from 3 to 20 minutes. Children's language was recorded by way of a portable audio recorder they wore in a vest. At the start of each observation the research assistant (who had spent one month in the classroom before beginning observations) asked the child to say his or her name and date into the tape recorder. The researcher then recorded the identity of the children and adults with whom the focal child interacted during that period.

Oral language was coded directly from the tapes onto coding sheets and scored according to the occurrence of cognitive and linguistic terms. Because of the varying durations of individual observation periods, relative scores were used. Variety of social contacts in the classroom (with children and adults) was also coded.

We also assessed children in a number of areas, including perspective taking, literacy and receptive vocabulary.

Cognitive perspective taking

Cognitive perspective taking was assessed following procedures outlined by Chandler (1973) where children responded to a series of five separate cartoons. Their response to each cartoon was rated (0, 3) according to their ability to divorce privileged from nonprivileged information; the unit of analysis was the mean of these five scores. Measurement was taken once, at the mid-point of the year.

Literacy

Literacy was assessed on a number of different fronts. First, children's phonological awareness, as a dimension of metalinguistic awareness, was measured using Bradley and Bryant's (1983) procedure. We administered this measure as a way in which to establish the validity of our claim that children's talk about language was a measure of metalinguistic awareness. If this was the case use of these terms should be positively and significantly correlated with the Bradley and Bryant measure.

Reading

Reading was measured in this study, as in the study reported in Chapter 4, with Clay's (1985) *Concepts about Print*. This measure was administered three times per year and we used the aggregate of children's scores to maximize reliability by reducing measurement variance (Rushton *et al.*, 1983).

Writing

Writing was assessed with two measures, both derived from Clay's (1985) battery. In the writing fluency measure children were asked to write as many words as they could; they were scored for the number of correctly spelled words they wrote. In the dictation procedure, children wrote a sentence dictated by an experimenter and they were scored for each phoneme correctly written. As with the reading measure, the aggregate score from the three administrations was used.

Vocabulary

Lastly, we used the Peabody Picture Vocabulary Test (Dunn and Dunn, 1981) as a measure of receptive vocabulary.

ta sources on the status of children's social experiences
l access to the information on the home lives of chil-
ne classroom, however (N=17). First, we utilized lit-
eracy diaries with children three times per week across the entire school
year. As part of the regular classroom regimen in one classroom children took a book of their choice and a journal home three times per
week. In the journal the following was recorded: the title of the book,
with whom they read the book, a response to the book, and the identity of the person making the response.

We noted a total of fourteen different participants in home literacy
events: mother, father, mother and father together, both plus a sibling,
grandfather, grandmother, both of them, older sibling, younger sibling,
male peer, female peer, baby sitter and target child. Our unit of analysis was the variety of participants in children's home literacy events as
recorded in these journals.

HOME Inventory

To determine the degree to which the variety measure was a valid indicator of the home environment, we correlated it with a reliable and
valid measure of quality of home environment, the HOME Inventory
(Caldwell and Bradley, 1984). The correlation was 0.66, $p<0.01$.

The HOME Inventory (Elementary) (Caldwell and Bradley, 1984)
was administered when the teacher and an assistant visited children
and their care providers in their home at the end of the school year.
The HOME is a widely used and valid measure of home environment
quality with regards to emotional and verbal responsivity, encourage-
ment of maturity, emotional climate, growth fostering materials and
experiences, provision for active stimulation, family participation,
paternal involvement and aspects of the physical environment.

Home literacy networks

Lastly, we constructed another measure of home literacy networks. We
developed this questionnaire, adapted from Cochran and Riley's (1988)
social network interview, to have adults identify the variety of different literacy events the child experienced at home as well as the variety of social participants in those events. This questionnaire was
administered by the classroom teacher as part of her parent confer-

ences during the spring of the school year. Again, we established the validity of this instrument as a measure of home environment quality by relating it to the HOME Inventory Total 1 score ($r=0.58$, $p<0.02$).

Results/discussion

Home social networks

We first present information on children's literacy events at home. Data from the three sources converge to suggest that children's experiences are rather restricted. Data from the teacher interviews of parents during the parent–teachers conferences revealed that the variety of events experienced ($M=1.36$), reading at bed time, writing letters, and the variety of participants in those events ($M=2.2$), e.g. mother and siblings, was rather limited.

Data from children's literacy diaries indicated that children often completed these alone. In cases where another person was present, this person was, in half of the cases, the child's mother, accounting for almost 60 percent of the cases where another participant was present. Fathers alone (1.4 percent) and fathers and mothers together (2.3 percent) were the next most common participants.

Next, we constructed a correlation matrix for all participants in children's literacy diaries. These correlations are displayed in Table 5.1. The analyses indicated that the frequency of being observed with mother alone was *negatively* correlated with other persons participating as well as a variety of other participants. Thus, when children interacted with mothers alone, others were excluded. When children's social networks are limited to their mothers it probably is indicative of a family under stress. Stress, in the form of economic hardships, hostile living environments and psychopathology, limits one's ability to establish and maintain supportive social contacts (Cochran and Riley, 1988). This interpretation is supported by the significant and negative correlation between frequency of mothers alone with the HOME total score ($r=-0.29$) and the positive correlation between variety of participants and the HOME total ($r=0.66$).

It should be noted that the interview and diary measures of variety were significantly intercorrelated ($r=0.58$). Also when we considered the stability of the variety of participants (as measured by the diaries) across the school year (by dividing the year in two parts) we found there to be no significant change. Thus, home environments are stable.

Table 5.1 Correlations among reading journal participants across the year

	2	3	4	5	6	7
Mother (1)	-0.23	-0.54**	-0.53**	-0.94**	-0.36	-0.58**
Father (2)		0.11	0.15	0.09	0.33	0.59**
Grandma (3)			0.88**	0.35	0.01	0.54**
Sibling (4)				0.36	-0.03	0.54**
Alone (5)					0.19	0.24
Mother and father (6)						0.70**
Variety (7)						

Note
** $p < 0.01$, one-tailed

School social networks and oral language

We begin by examining the continuity between home and school social networks. The correlation between variety of participants and literacy events in home literacy networks (as reported in the literacy network interview) and number of peers in school networks was significant (r=0.58, p<0.02). As hypothesized there was continuity between home and school. Children with diverse social contacts at home had diverse social contacts at school.

Children's perspective taking was significantly correlated with the number of peers (p<0.44, p<0.005) with whom children interacted with in their classrooms, not with adults (r=0.21, p ns). This relation is very consistent with Piagetian theory which suggests that interaction with peers, compared to adults, facilitates children's cognitive decentering.

The results among social perspective taking, social networks at home and social networks at school can be explained from a socialization or an individual difference perspective. The socialization argument holds that the experiences in diverse social contexts at home provide children with the opportunities to learn the skills necessary to interact with varied social actors in other venues, like school.

The individual difference point of view posits that some children are more sociable than others and this temperament predisposes them to seek out varied social contacts. We suggest that individual differences, like temperament, mediate socialization experiences. In subsequent chapters we will examine this proposition in more detail.

Next we examine variation in children's classroom oral across the school year. To this end we divide the school year into two time periods and test for differences. Descriptive statistics and ANOVA results are displayed in Table 5.2. First, we found that the variety of children's social contacts increased from time 1 to time 2; they interacted with more children and more adults as the year progressed. Similarly their use of literate language increased in frequency from time 1 to time 2. Not surprisingly children's social and linguistic performance increased during their first grade year.

We now consider the degree to which these forms of literate language related to school-based literacy.

Oral language and school-based literacy

Recall that we assessed literacy in terms of children's performance on Clay's (1985) *Concepts about Print* (CAP), Individual Word Writing

Table 5.2 Descriptive statistics for classroom interaction data

	Time 1		Time 2		F*	p
	M	SD	M	SD		
Adults	0.54	0.58	0.88	0.65	7.48	0.005
Peers	1.83	2.07	2.73	1.61	9.98	0.001
Past tense	0.41	0.50	0.60	0.40	2.20	ns
Future tense	0.0	0.01	0.14	0.20	8.36	0.003
Total tense	1.87	6.46	3.63	3.83	19.83	0.0001
3rd Person	0.15	0.13	0.13	0.10	4.90	0.02
CogT	0.22	0.31	0.14	0.16	0.94	ns
LingT	0.31	0.39	0.47	0.35	3.01	0.05
Total term	6.54	6.92	15.10	12.87	12.09	0.0005

Notes
CogT = Cognitive terms; LingT = Linguistic terms
*df = 1,30, one-tailed

Table 5.3 Intercorrelations among psychometric measures of literacy

	1	2	3	4	5
CAP (1)		0.76**	0.85**	0.71**	0.87**
PPVT (2)			0.63**	0.65**	0.71**
WORDWRIT (3)				0.65**	0.82**
B-B (4)					0.68**
DICWRIT (5)					

Notes
CAP = *Concepts about Print*; PPVT = Peabody Picture Vocabulary Test; WORDWRIT = Number of words written; B-B = Bradley and Bryant; DICWRIT = Words written in dictation task
**$p < 0.01$, one-tailed

Table 5.4 Correlations between decentering and oral language and literacy

	CAP	PPVT	WORDWRIT	DICWRIT	B-B
PT	0.49**	0.63**	0.40*	0.38*	0.51**
Past	0.36*	0.03	0.29	0.39*	0.27
Fut	0.04	0.21	-0.24	-0.14	-0.18
CogT	0.42**	0.34*	0.34*	0.55**	0.26
LingT	0.32*	0.33*	0.17	0.43**	0.40*
3rdP	0.32*	-0.11	0.20	-0.01	0.33

Notes
PT = Perspective taking; Past = Past tense; Fut = Future tense; CogT = Cognitive terms; LingT = Linguistic terms; 3rdP = 3rd person pronouns
*$p < 0.05$; **$p < 0.01$, one-tailed

Fluency, Dictation Writing and Bradley and Bryant's (1983) measure of phonological awareness. Children's performance on these measures was highly intercorrelated, as noted in Table 5.3. In keeping with our predictions and with the data from our preschool studies we found that children's use of metalanguage was significantly related to measures of reading and writing. These correlations are presented in Table 5.4. Further metalanguage was significantly related to the Bradley and Bryant (1983) measures of metalinguistic awareness, supporting our notion that use of these terms was indicative of children's reflection upon language.

These data also suggest that children's perspective taking ability was significantly correlated with measures of literate language and all measures of school-based literacy. This may indicate, as hypothesized, that literacy as measured by traditional psychometric instruments is a measure of children's ability to reflect upon language. Alternatively, it may mean that our perspective taking instrument is a measure of verbal facility, as well as a measure of perspective taking. Verbal facility is certainly important in early school based-literacy.

Conclusions/implications

In the data presented in this chapter we begin to more clearly specify those aspects of social context which might be important in early literacy learning. Motivated by Bernstein's (1960) socialization theory we found that variety of social contact related to children's cognitive decentering and literate language. Both of these constructs, in turn, related to standardized measures of literacy.

One reasonable interpretation for these results would be that contact with a varied social network at home facilitates children's cognitive decentering. The skill and strategies learned at home which lead to decentration were then used by children in their primary school classrooms.

Consistent with Olson's (1977) theory of literacy, these data can be conceptualized as the reflecting upon the linguistic and cognitive processes associated with literacy teaching. By way of qualification, however, we should note that the importance of metalanguage in children's learning to read and write in school may be an artifact of the way in which it is typically taught in school. Literacy is usually taught by decomposing words and text into their component parts and asking children to talk about them (Heath, 1983). Thus the ability to talk about language is an important dimension of the register of literacy teaching in schools as well as an important way in which it is assessed.

We next consider more closely dimensions of the social contexts which afford children's use of literate language. As noted above, variety of participants seemed to foster reflection upon language and thought processes. In the next chapter we consider the proposition that not all peers are equally supportive of children's use of literate language.

Chapter 6

Role of social relationships in literacy development

In the preceding chapters we saw how children's use of literate language was predictive of subsequent standardized measures of school-based literacy. From our perspective, a crucial aspect of literate language is the use of 'meta' talk, or talk about linguistic (e.g. 'This doll can't read!') and mental (e.g. 'I forgot to do that') states. The predictive power of talk about the mental and linguistic processes surrounding literacy teaching suggests that school-based literacy involves some level of cognitive decentering, or perspective taking.

We continue in this chapter to explicate dimensions of social context which afford children opportunities to decenter, and, consequently, to reflect upon cognitive and linguistic states. As we noted in the preceding chapters, researchers are only beginning to describe the social contexts which support children's use of literate language. Where social contextual effects on early literacy have been studied, the mother–child joint book reading context has been studied most extensively (e.g. Bus and vanIJzendoorn, 1995; Heath, 1983; Scarborough and Dobrich, 1994; Snow, 1983). As we saw in Chapters 4 and 5, preschool and young primary school children spend much of their time in and out of school with peers (Pellegrini *et al.*, 1995a).

Peer influences on cognitive development are often rooted in Piaget's (1983) equilibration theory where the conceptual conflict characteristic of complementary relations (or relations between two actors of equal status) spurs cognitive development. Research in the area of preschool children's symbolic play and its relation to literacy is an example of this line of work (Chapter 4). Researchers have found that the social and linguistic interaction between participants in pretend play settings is predictive of reading and writing status in the early primary grades (Dickinson and Moreton, 1991; Pellegrini and Galda, 1993). Also consistent with this Piagetian argument, in Chapter 5 we discussed how children's experience with varied social partners related to literate language and cognitive decentering. We proposed that experience with diverse partners, often with different points of view, provided children with opportunities to reflect upon the ways in which they conveyed meaning.

Peer relationships

This level of description of 'peer interaction' is probably still too global, because all peers are not equally facilitative of conceptual conflict/resolution and cognitive reflection. Different peer relationships, and their corresponding emotional dimensions, may be differentially important in this reflective process, and consequently, early literacy development. 'Relationship' here is defined as the interactional history between specific individuals that influences present and future interactions (Hinde, 1980). Thus, groups of peers may be characterized by different relationships, such as friends and acquaintances. The extent to which relationships are not typically considered in most theories of social influences on cognition leads us to believe that researchers consider relationships to be inconsequential; in most theories a peer is a peer. Where differences between peers are addressed, difference in peers' cognitive expertise, such as conservers and nonconservers (Murray, 1972), not relationships, is usually discussed.

Different relationships between participants do have implications for the specific of types of interactions that are relevant to literacy. Most generally, social interaction seems to relate to 'executive cognitive functioning' (Hartup, 1996; Wertsch, 1979), such as the ability to reflect upon language and cognitive processes. These processes are often observed in young children as they try to resolve conceptual conflicts with their playmates (Garvey and Shantz, 1992; Garvey and Kramer, 1989). Specific close relationships, like friendship and sibling relationships, may be especially important for the development of these 'meta' processes.

Friendships

Friendships are reciprocal, dyadic relationships (i.e. friends nominate each other as friends) and are characterized by strong emotional ties. This emotional component of peer contexts is crucial to consider in studies of social influences on literacy because it seems to support the exhibition of complex cognitive strategies (Dunn, 1988; Hartup, 1996), important to aspects of the development of literacy. Children who are friends, compared to children who are acquaintances, are emotionally invested in each other (Hartup, 1996) and the emotional tenor of friends' interactions supports the sorts of conceptual conflicts which afford opportunities to reflect upon cognitive and linguistic processes. This may be due to the fact that friends, compared to acquaintances, are less egotistic (Sullivan, 1953), are cooperative and complex players (Howes, 1993), are more task oriented, and deal with conflicts more constructively (Hartup, 1996) when they are with each other.

Specific to literacy learning, children with friends disagree and resolve disagreements. Because of their close and reciprocal ties, children often 'cool' the emotions that correspond to disagreement by verbally encoding their emotional states (Bruner, 1986). This cooling allows children to reflect upon the cognitive and linguistic processes constitutive of their interactions. These patterns, consistent with Piaget's (1983) theory, facilitate metacognitive and metalinguistic awareness which, in turn, should foster literacy learning (Pellegrini *et al.*, 1995a). The sparse extant data on friends, compared to acquaintances, interacting in literacy events support this argument (Daiute *et al.*, 1993; Jones and Pellegrini, 1996).

Task influences

In friendship, compared to acquaintance, situations we would expect children to engage in more cognitive conflicts and resolutions. These conflicts should also evidence the use of emotion terms. Further, the emotional tenor of friendship dyads should support higher levels of literate behavior, especially in demanding situations (Azimitia and Montgomery, 1993). For this reason we observed friend and acquaintance dyads as they interacted in a relatively demanding formal setting, writing a narrative with a peer, and a relatively informal setting, engaging in pretend play with narrative-eliciting props.

In this chapter, a formal setting is defined as one in which children are presented with a writing task by an adult. An informal task, on the other hand, is defined by the children themselves, not by an adult; pretend play is an example of an informal task. While the literate language generated in each of these peer settings predicts subsequent school-based literacy (Pellegrini and Galda, 1991; see also Chapters 4 and 5 this volume), there are important differences between more formal literacy learning methods, such as peer writing, and less formal methods, such as peer pretend play. Specifically, school writing lessons are usually associated with formal schooling and, consequently, are governed by *a priori* rules to which children must accommodate. Also, writing in most classrooms is usually serious business, partially because of these rules.

Play with peers, on the other hand, is not usually subject to the same teacher-imposed rules. Peer play is rule governed, but the rules are presented and negotiated between peers (Garvey, 1990) and are typically characterized by conceptual conflict and resolution cycles (Garvey and Kramer, 1989; Garvey and Shantz, 1992). In the process of these conflict resolution cycles children often talk about the emotions which characterize these conflicts. Talk about emotions has the effect of cooling those emotions and enabling children to reflect upon the linguistic and mental states around which the emotions center (Dunn, 1988; Garvey, 1990). When children disagree they talk also about the content and rationales for their opinions (Garvey, 1990; Pellegrini, 1984a). That children enjoy peer play, especially with friends, motivates them to sustain this difficult social cognitive work (Garvey, 1990).

The idea that young children exhibit higher levels of competence in pretense than in more serious school lessons is consistent with Vygotsky's (1978) theory of play. The theory posits that children's play scaffolds their exhibition of competence because in pretense they are motivated to reach fantastic goals, i.e. goals obtainable only through pretense, while simultaneously confronting themselves with rules governing these sorts of behaviors in real life (see Fein, 1979 for an excellent discussion of these issues).

In contrast, during peer writing, because it may be less motivating than peer play, children may choose not to expend much social cognitive effort to complete these tasks. Thus, formal literacy events, compared to peer pretend play, may actually suppress children's exhibition of competence while play may facilitate it (Vygotsky, 1978).

Gender

Children's gender is also relevant to the behavior children exhibit in pretend play and friendship settings. Girls are more skilled pretend players than boys (e.g. Fein, 1981; McLoyd, 1980) and consequently girls should exhibit higher levels of competence in the play context. Regarding friendship and gender, we know that children's friends are overwhelmingly of the same gender (Hartup, 1983) and that girls, more than boys, are more concerned with close relationships, such as friendship (Waldrop and Halverson, 1975). Thus, we expect girls to exhibit higher levels of competence in the friendship, compared to the acquaintance, condition.

While our knowledge of behaviors relevant to literacy learning in male and female friendship pairs is limited, we do have some general information which is helpful in generating hypotheses. For example, boys are more conflictual than girls (Maccoby, 1990). These differences are consistent with Maccoby's (1990) characterizations of interaction styles in gender segregated groups: girls are more enabling and emotional with each other while boys are more assertive.

Research goals

In this chapter we address a number of issues in the literature on social influences on early literacy development. First and most importantly, we further explicate the dimensions of social context, by comparing friend/acquaintance interactions, which relate to early literacy. Current conceptions of 'peer interaction' are much too global to further our understanding of social contexts supportive of literacy. Second, we determine the relative effects of formal (i.e. peer writing) and informal (i.e. peer play) instructional groupings on children's literate language. These two points provide complementary information on 'social contextual' effects on literacy learning. Third, we assess the degree to which these contexts relate to proximal and distal measures of literacy. By proximal measures of literacy we mean children's ability to write about the texts they were read and to re-read those texts. Distal measures of literacy were standardized measures of literacy.

We also expect the verbal interactional patterns elicited in friendship dyads to relate differentially to proximal and distal measures of literacy. To the extent that friendship dyads, compared to acquaintance dyads, support literacy learning and development we expect friends in the peer writing context to generate more sophisticated forms of writing and re-readings of texts while with their friends. Further, the oral language observed in the friendship context should relate to distal measures of literacy, such as performance on general measures of reading and writing.

While many studies of the oral language bases of literacy assess relations with distal measures of literacy (standardized test scores) this study took both distal and more proximal measures (assessment of reading and writing during the interactions). This should provide more concise information on the social bases of early literacy.

Methods

Subjects

The children who participated in the study were sampled from kindergarten classrooms in a public school in the southeastern USA. Individual classroom teachers were paid a small stipend ($100) for their participation in the study. A total of twenty-three girls and thirty-three boys participated. The mean age at the start of the study (September) was 65-months. African American children comprised 55 percent of the sample, European Americans 40 percent and other 5 percent.

Procedures

Children started kindergarten (which is mandatory in this state) in mid-August and attended school for the full day (7:50 a.m. to 2:30 p.m.), Monday through Friday, through the first week in June. After one month, graduate students started spending time in children's classrooms so that children would become familiar with them. Graduate students were assigned to classrooms in which to work. These graduate students were responsible for conducting all observational and initial sociometric/friendship sessions. Other research assistants were responsible for the second sociometric/friendship interviews and testing children; thus, observers were blind to children's status on the psychometric measures and testers were blind to children's behavioral status.

After approximately two weeks of researchers interacting with children in their classrooms so that they would be familiar with each other, researchers took individual students out of their classrooms and administered the initial sociometric and friendship nominations. In this procedure researchers placed individual pictures of children's classmates in front of them and said: 'I'm going to show you some pictures of your classmates. Please point to each and tell me the child's name.' When this was completed the researcher asked children (in the sociometric procedure) to 'Tell me the names of three children you like the most' and 'Three children you don't like.' The researcher wrote down names as they were given. Then the researcher asked the children: 'Who are some children in the class who are your friends?' Prompts, such as 'Who else?', 'Are there others?', were used. This procedure, administered by a research assistant unfamiliar with children's earlier nominations, was repeated again in May of the school year. Based on the friendship nominations, friend/non-friend dyads were constructed. Friends were defined, following Hartup (1996), as children with reciprocal friendship nominations; that is, children were friends when they nominated each other as friends. Acquaintances were non-friends from the same classroom. All dyads were comprised of same gender, same race children.

Children were observed in friendship or acquaintance dyads twelve times across the school year; six times in a play setting (informal) and six times in a peer writing setting (formal). The separate play observations involved replica toys from currently popular narrative films: *Aladdin*, *The Jungle Book* and *The Lion King*. The formal setting involved children being read a book by an experimenter and then asked to talk and write about the book. Books were all narratives related to the theme of birthdays: G. Clark's (1992) *How Many Days to My Birthday?*, C. Rylant's (1987) *Birthday Presents*, and M. Brown's (1989) *Arthur's Birthday*. Order of presentation of play (informal)/ peer writing (formal) and friend/non-friend contexts was counterbalanced, with one exception, across classrooms and three academic quarters. The one exception related to the initial presentation of the books in the writing setting. Because of new kindergarteners' limited literacy skills, the simplest book was presented first (*How Many Days to My Birthday?*).

Children were observed at tables in a hall outside their classrooms. In all cases researchers placed an audio recorder on the table. Before each session began the researcher announced the date, children's names and the condition. Measures of children's oral language and duration (in seconds) of the episode were derived from the audio recordings.

In the writing setting researchers first read the assigned book to the group. After each book, researchers followed standardized instructions to encourage children to talk and write about the stories they had just heard. Children's written products from these sessions were subsequently scored in terms of level of writing performance; scoring is discussed below. At the end of each quarter, children were individually asked to re-read to the researcher the book they had read in the earlier writing session.

In the play contexts, children were presented with the replica props and encouraged to play. In each setting researchers were minimally intrusive; they sat off to the side of the play area. Additionally, over the course of the year a number of language and literacy assessment instruments were administered.

Measures

Measures of children's oral language production during play and literacy events were taken, as were measures of children's reading and writing.

Language production

Measures of children's oral language were derived from the audio recordings of the play and literacy observational sessions. Oral language tapes were coded by one of the research assistants according to mutually exclusive categories. All measures of oral language derived from audiotapes were expressed in terms of relative frequency (relative to the sum of all coded utterances for each observation).

Conjunctions were coded as additive (e.g. *and*), temporal (e.g. *and then*), causal (e.g. *because*) or adversative (e.g. *but*). Linguistic, cognitive and emotional verbs were coded as regular and contrastive. Use of linguistic (e.g. ***Talk*** *louder*), cognitive (e.g. *Let me* ***think***) and emotional (e.g. *I'm* ***happy*** *now*) terms indicates children's knowledge of those processes (Pellegrini *et al.*, 1995a). Lastly, contrastive linguistic (e.g. *You* ***can't say*** *that*), cognitive (e.g. *It* ***doesn't make sense***) and emotion terms (e.g. *He's* ***not really sad***) are most indicative of reflection on the processes they encode (Shatz *et al.*, 1983) and predictive of early literacy (Pellegrini and Galda, 1991).

Names of letters and literacy artifacts were also coded. Any mention of a letter name or object associated with literacy (e.g. book, pencil, paper) was coded. Rhymes and word play were also coded. This category included instances of singing, reciting poems or rhyming words.

Lastly, oral language tapes were coded for disagreements and make-ups. Disagreements included any mention of disbelief, disagreement, efforts to substitute one thing for another, postponements and evasions. Make-ups were represented by compromise, expression of sorrow/apology, accepting explanation/alternative.

Literacy

Children's literacy (reading and writing) was measured on a number of instruments. Distal reading measures included Clay's (1985) *Concepts about Print*, which was administered twice a year: one form (*Stones*) in the fall and another form (*Sand*) in the spring. Standard scores on the aggregate of these measures were used. Also at these sessions children took the letter recognition and word recognition subtests, as well as the word writing fluency measure. All testing was done by a trained school psychologist. All of these aggregated measures are regarded as distal measures of literacy.

More proximally, children's reading was also assessed three times per year by their re-reading a children's book. Specifically, at the end of each of the three academic quarters individual children were asked to re-read the book that they played about that quarter to the researchers. Children's re-reading was audiotaped and coded according to Pellegrini and Galda's (1991) reconceptualization of Sulzby's (1987) categorization of re-reading. Briefly, children re-read the book and the various strategies they used in this process were coded on a 1–11 continuum. The categories were as follows:

1　Labeling pictures
2　Action governed descriptions of pictures
3　Disconnected dialogue where children use some pictures to tell the story
4　Stories told for audience where stories around pictures are cohesive
5　Created story where pictures are used to tell a different story
6　Story similar to written version but not verbatim
7　Verbatim-like attempts where children point to pictures and tell verbatim story
8　Print governed refusal where children say they can't read
9　Aspectual attempts where children use one or more of the following to re-read: letter/sound attempts, read known words, and try to recite text from memorized words
10　Strategy dependent attempts where one of the above strategies (in 9) represents a majority of the strategies used
11　Independent reading.

Children's use of individual strategies across the whole reading were considered. The highest score on the re-reading was used in analyses. It correlated positively and significantly with Clay's *Concepts about Print* total score ($r = 0.27$, $p < 0.04$) and the Word Identification scores ($r = 0.28$, $p < 0.03$).

Writing was measured in two ways. First, at the distal level and as part of the administration of the *Concepts about Print* measure in the fall and spring of the year, children were also asked to write individual words. Following procedures outlined by Clay children were told:

'I want to see how many words you can write. Can you write your name?' If children refused or said 'No', they were asked to write any single-letter or two-letter words. If children could write their name, they were told: 'Good. Now let's think of all the words you know how to write and write them down.' Standardized prompts, following Clay (1985), were used. Each word written in standardized form was counted as correct and the unit of analysis was the total score correct. This measure has high reliability and validity (Clay, 1985).

The second, more proximal, measure of writing performance was derived from the children's written products generated after being read to in the literacy conditions. Each written product was scored according to Pellegrini and Galda's adaptation of Sulzby's (1987) continuum of writing development. Each piece was scored 1–6 on the following criteria, for the highest level exhibited:

1   Drawing: children drew pictures of the story, with no words or letter present
2   Scribbling: children used curved lines, not words
3   Letter-like units: children used graphic signs, like squares, triangles and circles, to represent words
4   Well-learned units: children repeated the use of individual letters, e.g. AAA, ZZ
5   Invented spelling: children used their own spelling for individual words
6   Conventional orthography: children used conventional spelling

This score correlated 0.62, $p < 0.01$, with the Clay measure of writing fluency.

Results/discussion

We present, respectively, data from the observational sessions and children's scores on literacy measures. For the observational data the dyad, not the individual child, was the unit of analysis. This was done for two reasons. First, we were interested in relationships, not individuals; thus dyads are the appropriate unit of analysis. Second, individuals interacting in dyads are statistically interdependent and to use individual, not dyad, scores violates independence assumptions of parametric statistics as well as increases the chances of Type 1 error.

Variation in the observational data

In the first series of analyses we examine the effects of gender (2), social context (2: friend/acquaintance) and formality context (2: play/peer writing) on children's oral language production. The first two factors are between-subjects variables and the last factor was a within-subjects variable. These analyses are generally concerned with children's use of literate language (conjunctions, cognitive, linguistic, literate and letter terms, and rhymes), and emotion language (emotion terms and disagreements/make-ups). Again, these values are relative scores for dyads of children; one-tailed tests were used because of *a priori* hypotheses.

Conjunctions were analyzed first and for additive conjunctions, a significant social context and gender interaction ($F(1–15)=4.90$, $p<0.02$) was observed such that girls generated more in the friend condition ($M=0.025$) than in the acquaintance condition ($M=0.02$) and boys ($M=0.03$) generated more than girls in that latter condition as well. For temporal conjunctions no significant effects were observed. For causal conjunctions a significant effect for social context ($F(1–15)=7.45$, $p<0.005$), and a significant social context and gender interaction ($F(1–15)=5.87$, $p<0.01$), were observed. Like the additive results, girls generated more causal conjunctions with friends ($M=0.015$) than with acquaintances ($M=0.01$). Further, in the friend condition, they generated more causals than boys ($M=0.01$).

For the cognitive terms a significant effect for gender ($F(1–15)=8.20$, $p<0.005$) was observed, with girls ($M=0.03$) using more cognitive terms than boys ($M=0.015$). For the cognitive contrast terms a significant effect for social context was observed ($F(1–15)=4.08$, $p<0.03$), where more were observed between friends ($M=0.01$) than acquaintances ($M=0.001$).

For linguistic terms significant main effects were observed for the formal/play condition ($F(1–15)=56.53$, $p<0.0001$) and the social context ($F(1–15)=14.76$, $p<0.0001$). More linguistic terms were observed in peer writing ($M=0.04$) than in play ($M=0.015$), while more linguistic terms were observed in the friend dyads ($M=0.035$) than in the acquaintance dyads ($M=0.02$). Regarding linguistic contrast terms a main effect was observed in the formal/play condition ($F(1–15)=11.35$, $p<0.002$), with more being observed in the formal condition ($M=0.01$) than in the play condition ($M=0.005$).

Next, we analyzed the effects of gender (2) and social context (2) and formality context (2) on names of letters, names of literacy artifacts and rhymes. For each variable, respectively, a significant main effect for formality was observed: ($F(1–15)=27.02$, $p<0.0001$; $F(1–15)=5.0$, $p<0.04$; $F(1–15)=42.42$, $p<0.0001$). In the respective cases of letter names ($M=1.75$ and $M=0.01$), literacy artifacts ($M=2.75$ and $M=0.01$) and rhymes ($M=0.01$ and $M=0.002$), more terms were observed in the formal setting than in the informal setting.

For emotion terms no significant effects were observed. For emotion contrast terms a significant effect for gender ($F(1–15)=6.81$, $p<0.005$) was observed where girls ($M=0.013$) used more than boys ($M=0.01$).

Next we consider disagreements and make-ups (conflict resolution cycles). Regarding, disagreements, a significant gender effect ($F(1–15)=5.91$, $p<0.01$: boys, $M=0.032$ and girls, $M=0.02$) was observed as was a significant effect for the writing ($M=0.017$)/play ($M=0.035$) setting ($F(1–15)=12.94$, $p<0.001$).

Change in friendship nominations

Next we examined children's change in friendship choices from fall to spring of the school year. Specifically, we tested the hypothesis that children paired with non-friends at the beginning of the year would nominate those same children as friends at the end of the year. This hypothesis was tested, using the large sample approximation of Fisher's sign test (Hollander and Wolfe, 1973), by examining the probability of a non-friend partner in the fall being chosen as a friend in the spring. The hypothesis was supported; non-friends became friends in 72 percent of the cases ($B=3.35$, $p<0.005$).

Relations between emotion, cognitive and linguistic language

First, the observational measures of emotion language (i.e. emotion language and disagree/make-up) were positively intercorrelated. These correlations are displayed in Table 6.1.

In the next series of analyses we determined the extent to which children's use of emotion language (i.e. the aggregate of emotion terms, emotion contrast terms and disagree/make-ups) predicted cognitive language (i.e. the aggregate of cognitive terms and cognitive contrast terms) and linguistic language (i.e. the aggregate of linguistic terms and linguistic contrast terms). Aggregation was justified in light of the significant intercorrelations among the measures. Further, aggregation

Table 6.1 Correlations among social emotional variables

	2	3	4
EmoTerms (1)	0.40**	0.43**	0.20*
EmoContrast (2)		0.39**	0.34**
Disagree (3)			0.59**
Makeup (4)			

Notes
EmoTerms = Emotional terms; EmoContrast = Contrastive emotional terms; Disagree = Disagreements; Makeup = Makeup (resolution) of disagreement
*$p<0.05$, **$p<0.01$

is helpful in maximizing construct validity for developmental variables, such as early literacy (Rushton *et al.*, 1983). We were interested in the extent to which emotion language was mediated by the interaction between gender and social context (friend/non-friend condition) in predicting cognitive and linguistic language. Using hierarchic regression analyses emotion language predicted a significant portion of the variance in both cognitive ($R^2=0.23$, $p<0.0001$) and linguistic language ($R^2=0.46$, $p<0.0001$); the gender and friend/non-friend condition did not account for significant variance when entered into the equation either before or after emotion language.

Relations between language and literacy variables

The language measures were significantly intercorrelated as were the literacy measures; thus the language measures are labeled 'literate language' and the literacy measures are labeled 'literacy'. These correlations are displayed in Tables 6.2 and 6.3.

Correlations in Table 6.4 between oral language variables and measures of literacy reveal a rather clear pattern. Specifically oral language which encoded linguistic processes and terms associated with literacy events were reliably related to literacy. Terms encoding more general cognitive processes were less likely to be related to literacy.

Predicting literacy

In the next series of analyses, hierarchic regression techniques were used to predict an aggregate literacy score (the aggregate of the *Concepts about Print*, Word Identification and Word Writing scores). Aggregation, again, is justified in light of the significant intercorrela-

Table 6.2 Correlations among cognitive, linguistic and literacy oral language variables

	2	3	4	5	6	7	8	9	10
Conjunc									
Add (1)	0.63**	0.65**	0.66**	0.22	0.50**	0.05	0.12	0.21	0.22
Temp (2)		0.74**	0.55**	0.45**	0.64**	0.17	0.30*	0.51**	0.21
Caus (3)			0.43**	0.37**	0.14	0.01	0.27*	0.70**	0.18
Cognitive									
Terms (4)				0.41**	0.44**	0.18	0.06	0.18	0.37**
Contrast (5)					0.51**	0.23	0.40**	0.43**	0.03
Linguistic									
Terms (6)						0.36**	0.42**	0.72**	0.13
Contrast (7)							0.19	0.31**	0.35**
Literacy									
LetterName (8)								0.47*	0.05
ArtefactName (9)									0.09
Rhymes (10)									

Notes
*p<0.05; **p<0.01

Table 6.3 Correlations among literacy measures

	2	3	4	5
WORDWRIT (1)	0.50**	0.74**	0.31*	0.62**
CAP (2)		0.52**	0.26*	0.38**
WordId (3)			0.31*	0.28*
Highest read (4)				0.27*
Highest write (5)				

Notes
WORDWRIT = Number of words written; CAP = *Concepts about Print*; WordId = Word identification; Highest read = Highest score on the re-read scale; Highest write = Highest score on the writing scale
*p<0.05; **p<0.01

tion among the measures. Predictor measures included the following oral language: cognitive language (aggregate of cognitive terms and cognitive contrast terms), linguistic language (aggregate of linguistic terms and linguistic contrast terms) and literate terms (the aggregate of names of letters and artifacts, as well as rhymes). Gender and friend/non-friend condition was used as an interaction term. The model

Table 6.4 Correlation coefficients between oral language and literacy

	Cognitive		Ling		Literate terms		
	Term	Cont	Term	Cont	Nam	Artef	Rhym
Proximal							
Read	0.06	0.27*	0.22*	0.05	0.31**	0.36**	0.20
Write	0.10	0.23*	0.10	0.10	0.30**	0.08	0.01
Distal							
Write	0.09	0.07	0.30**	0.29**	0.10	0.32**	0.13
CAP	0.02	0.10	0.11	0.31**	0.05	0.10	0.01
Wordld	0.19	0.01	0.28*	0.21	0.11	0.23*	0.11

Notes
*$p<0.05$; **$p<0.01$

accounted for 9 percent ($R^2=0.09$, $p<0.03$) of the variance in literacy, linguistic language was the only significant predictor. Even when cognitive language was entered before linguistic language, cognitive language did not account for significant variance (contributed less than 1 percent of the variance).

In the last regression model we entered emotion language first, and then allowed cognitive and linguistic language. Neither emotion nor cognitive terms contributed significantly to literacy.

General discussion

Early literacy researchers are currently interested in the social contexts of learning. In this chapter, in conjunction with Chapter 5, we have extended this line of inquiry by explicating more clearly different dimensions of social contexts and the ways in which they relate to literacy learning. Most basically, we have demonstrated the importance of further differentiating aspects of the 'peer context'. As we have stressed, not all peers are equally facilitative of literacy learning. Methodologically, our work extends the important observations of Kramer and colleagues (1989) who found that individual children's language varied in different peer dyads. They suggested that each dyad presents individuals with a unique context in which to function. While we agree with Kramer and colleagues (1989) that the dyad is an interactive unit, we add that the relationship between individuals within dyads is implicated in the interaction processes.

The differences between peers in dyads may be related to the emotional tenor of their relationships. Specific peer relationships, like friendship, support literate language to the extent that friends, compared to acquaintances, are emotionally committed to each other. This emotional tenor is realized in children's use of emotional terms and conflicts/make-ups with friends. Expression of emotion is related to children's use of emotion terms and literate language. Literate language, in turn, predicted literacy status, as measured by a battery of measures developed by Marie Clay. In short, close relationships, like friendship, support synchronous and cognitively complex interactions. The emotional tenor of these relationships affords children opportunities to reflect upon cognitive and linguistic processes which constitute early literacy (Dunn, 1988; Hartup, 1996).

Further, our predictions for gender and social context interactions were, generally, supported. Close relationships for girls, compared to boys, afforded opportunities to express literate language. This finding is consistent with extant literature documenting girls' concern with close relationships (Maccoby, 1990; Waldrop and Halverson, 1975). Also consistent with this literature was the finding that boys were more conflictual than girls.

These results extend our current understanding of social context and learning. At the most basic level researchers should attend to the nature of relationships between peers, and indeed between children and adults (e.g. Bus and vanIJzendoorn, 1988). Relationships between participants in dyads could be partially responsible for the observed variability of child language with different peers (Kramer *et al.*, 1989). We noted differences when children were observed with friends, compared with acquaintances.

Complicating this picture of 'social context' further was the fact that children who started off as acquaintances, but not friends, became friends by the end of the school year. Young children who are not initially friends seem to become friends when they share the same environment. Thus, friendship, for young children at least, is related to propinquity (Hartup, 1983). For older children, friendship is based on other factors, such as shared interests and self disclosure (Hartup, 1983).

The formality of the interactional setting also influenced language between peers. Formality was defined in terms of a contrast between typical 'school' tasks (in the form of peer writing assignments made by an adult) and peer pretend play. Formality of task effects was observed only for linguistic terms. Children generated more of these terms when they interacted in the formal literacy setting than in the informal pretend play setting. This should not be surprising to the extent that the formal setting was a literacy setting and children verbally encoded aspects of that environment. That these were the same terms that also predicted literacy supports Olson's (1977) contention that school-based literacy is something that must be taught; it is not usually learned incidentally. Our data suggest that teaching includes providing children with society's artifacts for school literacy and having them use them with their peers.

This is not to say, however, that pretend play with peers does not support the use of literate language. Both theory (Piaget, 1983; Vygotsky, 1978) and the empirical record (Pellegrini, 1984b) suggest that the role of pretend play in early literacy is important during the preschool and early primary grade periods. It may be the case, following practice theories of play (Fein, 1979; Piaget, 1983), that pretend play with peers helps children consolidate the literate language learned in other contexts. This seems to be the case for preschoolers who learn literate language in joint reading events with a parent and then use these forms with peers in pretense (Pellegrini and Galda, 1991).

Lastly, we discuss the ways in which observed language variables (i.e. cognitive, linguistic and emotion language) predicted children's literacy status. These results are rather clear cut and consistent with theory (e.g. Olson, 1977). Talk about language and literacy was a reliable predictor of literacy. Talk about other mental states does not add significantly to that prediction. This finding replicates earlier research implicating talk about language and literacy events and rhyming in formal literacy attainment (Bradley and Bryant, 1983; Torrance and Olson, 1984; Pellegrini and Galda, 1991). Children's rhyming and talk about language is an indicator of their general metalinguistic awareness, as well as their phonemic awareness (Pellegrini *et al.*, 1995a). Children's phonemic awareness is a robust predictor of early reading status (Adams, 1990).

That children's use of emotion language was not directly implicated in predicting literacy also merits discussion. It seems that emotion language was indirectly implicated to the extent that it related significantly to children's use of literate language, which, in turn, related directly to literacy. Emotion, in the form of expression of emotions and conflict resolution cycles, provides the emotional tenor that supports children's reflection upon language and literacy. This explanation is consistent with Piaget's (1983) equilibration theory as well as Dunn's (1988) more recent observations of children interacting in another close relationship, with siblings.

Conclusion/implications

This chapter, along with Chapter 5, represents initial efforts to explicate 'social context' and its effect on literacy learning. We have shown that distinctions such as 'peer context' are much too global. Different sorts of peer relations and different sorts of instructional settings affect children's interactions and subsequent learning. Future research should look toward making clearer distinctions among peers. For example, we might expect 'best friend' relationships to be more supportive than other more general friends. The observation of Kramer *et al.* (1989) that children's language varies according to dyadic context is an important one. Not only do we need to sample individuals in different dyadic contexts, as suggested by Kramer *et al.* (1989), but also we need to understand the nature of relationships of the peers constituting those dyads. Hinde's (1980) relationships model and Lerner's (1984) developmental contextual model provide important guides for this sort of research. In both cases, individuals, and their unique characteristics, are considered in different relationships. That relationships are affected by individual differences is important for future research to consider. The sibling literature can provide important guidance in this area. For example, siblings' temperaments affect their relationships with each other, as well as other interaction patterns (e.g. Brody *et al.*, 1994). In Chapter 7 we consider the ways in which differences in children's temperaments affect their interactions in different social arrangements.

Chapter 7

Relationships, individual differences, and children's use of literate language

In Chapter 6, like many other researchers, we demonstrated the facilitative effects (Sackett *et al.*, 1981) of different social contexts on children's cognitive processes (e.g. Bus and vanIJzendoorn, 1995; Hartup, 1996). In our two previous chapters on peer influences on children's use of literate language, we have demonstrated the supportive nature of both diverse and close peer contacts.

'Meta' talk occurs frequently in the context of peers' and friends' conceptual conflicts and resolutions (Pellegrini, 1985). The conflict-resolution process often has children taking a peer's utterance, and then talking about it (Pellegrini, 1985). Consider the following example from two preschoolers playing with a doll and a doctor's kit.

A: Ooo. There's poo all on her diaper.
J: Doctors can't say poo.
A: Poo?
J: It's a naughty word.
A: **Doctors** can say poo.

In this case two children disagree about situational appropriateness of word choice. In the process of the disagreement, they talk about linguistic processes *per se*. The fact that they talk about talk indicates that they are reflecting on the process (Dunn, 1988; Pellegrini *et al.*, 1995a).

Friends, compared to non-friends, frequently disagree and resolve disagreements (Hartup, 1996). This may be due to the fact that friends are emotionally invested in each other. That they like and trust each other leads them, as noted above, to monitor these conflicts closely. Evidence that friends monitor the emotional dimensions of conflicts comes from the observation that these conflicts are often accompanied by expression of emotion terms, e.g. *naughty*, *sad*, *happy*, suggesting that children are reflecting upon their feelings and those of their friends (Slomkowski and Dunn, 1993). The use of these emotional terms may also indicate that they are using language to 'cool' their emotions (Bruner, 1986). This cooling may be necessary for children to reflect upon the social and linguistic dimensions of the conflict/resolution (Bruner, 1986; Dunn, 1988).

We suggest that these conflict/resolution cycles and their subsequent encoding of emotional terms should facilitate the sorts of metacognitive and metalinguistic awareness which are constitutive of literate language (Pellegrini *et al.*, 1995a; Piaget, 1983).

The nature of the interactions in friend and non-friend groupings, as we saw in Chapter 6, is mediated by factors such as children's gender and temperament. The literature is quite clear on gender differences in interaction styles: boys are assertive and conflictual and girls are enabling and emotionally expressive (Maccoby, 1990). More specific to interaction styles embedded within relationships, girls, more than boys, are concerned with close relationships, such as friendship (Waldrop and Halverson, 1975). Thus, we expect friendship contexts to support girls' expression of emotions more than non-friendship contexts.

In order to more clearly understand interactions within different relationships, we must also consider the contributions made by different individuals (Hinde, 1978). Consideration of individual differences is noticeably absent from most discussions of social context and early literacy learning. We suggest that children, as well as older individuals, enter into relationships in different ways. These differences affect the social contexts into which individuals select themselves and the ways in which they interact with others. To ignore the role of individual differences in social interaction implies that individuals are passive recipients of larger socialization forces. This, as Tooby and Cosmides (1992) have argued, is to reduce children's development to a unidirectional, social reproduction process. Consideration of individual differences enables us to make provision for individuals' contribution to the interaction process; consequently development can be studied as a transactional, not unidirectional, process.

Individual differences are often operationalized in terms of children's temperament. Temperament refers to individuals' behavioral style, especially as it relates to emotional responses, and is related to biological make-up; consequently temperament is expressed very early in children's development and is stable across childhood (Campos *et al.*, 1983). The ways in which emotionality is expressed have clear implications for interpersonal interaction and relationships. For example, active and intense children tend to play interactively with peers (Hinde *et al.*, 1985). At the relationship level, 'difficult children' (e.g. high levels of physical activity and emotionally intense) may exhibit more conflicts, especially when they are interacting with children with whom they are not close. Being with a friend, on the other hand, may attenuate conflicts for these children.

Taken together, temperament and gender probably affect expression of emotions in different social arrangements. Conflict/resolution cycles should lead to expression of emotions, both of which should affect literate language. We view friendship, compared to acquaintance, contexts as more supportive of literate language expression.

The separate conceptual models for friendship and acquaintance conditions are presented in Figure 7.1.

This model extends current thinking about social influences on the development of cognitive processes by examining in concert previously unexplored dimensions of social context, relationships and temperament.

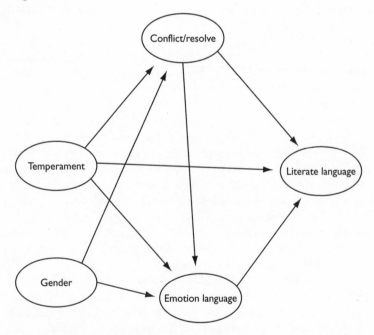

Figure 7.1 Influence of temperament and gender mediated by emotion language and conflict/resolution on literate language (model)

In summary, we present an extended model of the ways in which peers interact in a literacy learning context. As we noted in Chapter 6, children's friendships support the sort of interaction which leads to the use of literate language. For example, conceptual conflicts and resolutions afford opportunities to reflect upon language and thought processes.

In this chapter we extend Chapter 6 in two ways. First, we present and test this model as a process. Second, we consider the extent to which different types of children interact in friendship and non-friendship conditions. It is probably the case that different types of children interact differently in different peer groups.

Methods

Participants and procedures

In this chapter we simply re-analyzed the data collected in Chapter 6; thus the subjects and all procedures are identical to those in Chapter 6. All oral language measures were also defined and coded in the same way. We will, however, explain the temperament instrument used in this study as it was not reported above.

Temperament was assessed with Martin's (1988) Temperament Assessment Battery (TAB)-Teacher Form. Teachers completed this 48-item instrument on each child in January of the school year. The TAB has six empirically verified factors (Martin *et al.*, 1988): activity (motoric vigor), adaptability (speed and ease in which child adjusts to new situation), approach/withdraw (approaches or withdraws from social interaction in the first encounter with a new social situation), intensity (vigor of emotional intensity), distractibility (tendency to divert to non-task stimuli) and persistence (attention span and continues with difficult learning tasks). Only the scores from the activity, emotional intensity, and distractibility factors were utilized because preliminary analyses (principal components analyses) suggested that only they were empirically interrelated as a factor.

Results/discussion

Means and standard deviations for all study variables are displayed in Table 7.1. As in Chapter 6, the data are grouped by dyad. Separate variables for individual measures of literate language, emotion language, conflicts/resolutions and dimensions of temperament were

Table 7.1 Means and standard deviations for study variables

	Friends		Non-friends	
	Mean	SD	Mean	SD
Temperament				
Activity	30.62	9.76	32.50	9.19
EmoInten	30.82	7.53	31.41	7.30
Distract	34.97	9.03	36.34	9.36
Emotion language*				
EmoTerms	0.08	0.09	0.07	0.06
EmoContrast	0.01	0.02	0.01	0.02
Conflict/resolution*				
Conflict	0.64	0.41	0.56	0.30
Resolution	0.09	0.07	0.08	0.06
Literate language*				
CogTerms	0.28	0.23	0.25	0.17
CogContrast	0.05	0.04	0.04	0.04
LingTerms	0.46	0.27	0.40	0.24
LingContrast	0.03	0.03	0.03	0.03
ArtefactTerms	0.25	0.21	0.26	0.19

Note
* Expressed in relative frequencies

considered manifest variables. Manifest variables within each category (e.g. literate language and temperament) were aggregated into separate latent variables. The intercorrelations of the manifest variables within each of these latent variables are displayed in Table 7.2.

Structural equation modeling with partial least squares (PLS) was employed to test the model presented in Figure 7.1. This procedure was developed for situations which do not meet the restrictive assumptions of maximum likelihood techniques, such as LISREL (Falk and Miller, 1991). An important advantage of PLS is that it assesses direct and indirect effects, both of which are included in our model. Goodness of fit indices assess the degree to which the hypothesized model reproduces the actual covariation matrix. The coefficient RMS COV, or root mean square of the covariance between the residuals of the manifest and latent variables (E,U), is an index of the model's fit with the data. A coefficient of 0 indicates that the model and data match with complete accuracy; a coefficient above 0.20 is indicative of a poor model, and a coefficient of 0.02 is superior. The coefficients for our friend model was 0.06 and for our non-friend model was 0.07, indicating good fits.

Table 7.2 Intercorrelations manifest variables within each latent variable

Temperament

	2	3
Activity (1)	0.64*	0.84*
EmoInten (2)		0.71*
Distract (3)		

Emotion language

	2
EmoTerms (1)	0.40*
EmoContrast (2)	

Conflict/resolution

	2
Conflict (1)	0.59*
Resolution (2)	

Literate language

	2	3	4	5
CogTerms (1)	0.41*	0.44*	0.18	0.18
CogContrast (2)		0.51*	0.23	0.43*
LingTerms (3)			0.36*	0.72*
LingContrast (4)				0.31*
ArtefactTerms (5)				

Note
* $p < 0.01$

The PLS program uses composite weights in creating latent variables. The procedure also optimizes linear relations between predictor and predicted components. Paths between the constructs in the model are standardized path coefficients (*beta* weights). Differences were observed such that the friend model accounted for more variance than the non-friend model.

To reduce data, manifest variables are combined into theoretical components, or latent variables. The factor loadings, which are approximations of first principal component loadings, of the manifest variables on latent constructs are presented in Table 7.3. The overall variance accounted for in the measurement models for the friend and non-friend conditions, respectively, were (h^2) 0.73 and 0.70. The R^2 for the friends and non-friends models for friends and non-friends were statistically significant (see Figure 7.2). Generally, the models fit the data very well.

To eliminate the possibility that the differences between the models were due to sample differences, not differences in the relationships between participants, we tested group differences in temperament and

Table 7.3 Loading pattern matrices for friends and non-friends

	Friends				Non-friends			
	1	2	3	4	1	2	3	4
Temperament								
Activity	0.95				0.95			
EmoInten	0.77				0.80			
Distract	0.94				0.94			
Emotion language								
EmoTerms		0.96				0.95		
EmoContrast		0.95				0.85		
Conflict/resolution								
Conflict			0.93				0.78	
Resolution			0.80				0.81	
Literate language								
CogTerms				0.72				0.47
CogContrast				0.67				0.74
LingTerms				0.92				0.91
LingContrast				0.71				0.72
ArtefactTerms				0.73				0.83

literate language. This was accomplished by multiplying the raw score for each measure by its latent weight and then conducting t-tests between the groups; no differences were observed for either temperament ($t=1.20$, $p=0.88$) or literate language ($t=1.02$, $p=0.93$).

In the model for the friend dyads, temperament had a direct effect on emotion language, conflict/resolutions and literate language. As hypothesized, active and emotionally intense children expressed more emotion and engaged in more conflicts and resolutions. The effect of temperament on literate language was also mediated by emotion language and conflict/resolutions. Conflict/resolutions predicted emotion language and both of these variables had direct effects on literate language: expression of emotion terms and conflicts and resolutions, as hypothesized, predicted literate language.

Gender directly affected emotion language and conflict/resolutions: boys were likely to engage in conflict/resolution cycles while girls were not. For expression of emotions, boys expressed more emotion than girls. As noted above, our model predicted 0.69 of the variance in literate language.

The non-friend model was different from the friend model in a number of important ways. First, and most importantly, the latter model

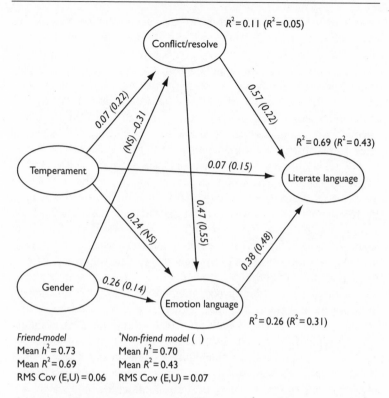

Figure 7.2 Influence of temperament and gender mediated by emotion language and conflict/resolution on literate language (significance data)

accounted for substantially less variance in literate language than the former. Second, temperament did not predict expression of emotion language; it did predict conflicts/resolutions, as in the friend model. Third, gender did not predict conflict/resolutions.

In this chapter we extended extant knowledge of social influences on early literacy learning by extending our conceptualization of the peer context of learning. To date, most studies of peer influences on literacy learning have been rather global, not considering relationships or individuals' contributions to interactions. To our knowledge, no one has considered how these dimensions of social context affect early literacy behavior in concert.

In Chapter 6 we demonstrated the importance of differentiating aspects of 'peer context' in terms of those peers' relationships. As we have stressed, not all peers are equally facilitative of learning. Important differences in the ways in which peers interact in dyads are related to boys' and girls' individual differences and close relationships. Specific peer relationships, like friendship, support literate language to the extent that friends, compared to acquaintances, are emotionally committed to each other. This commitment facilitates friends' monitoring of their social interactions which is evidenced by their use of emotional terms (Dunn and Slomkowski, 1992).

Individual differences of participants also affect interactions in different relationships. With non-friends an active, emotionally intense temperament leads to conflicts and resolutions, not expression of emotion terms. With friends, this sort of temperament leads to conflicts and resolutions as well as expression of emotion terms. Thus, friendship seems to support expression of emotion terms between 'difficult' children (Martin et al., 1988). By implication, the friendship context seems to support difficult children's reflecting upon their social interactions and emotional states during peer interactions. These results support more general descriptions of interactions between friends as being conflictual as well as emotionally supportive (Hartup, 1996). Future research should explore the specific sorts of conflicts and resolutions and their corresponding emotional states (Arsenio and Killen, 1996). It may be the case that low levels of conflict affect expression of positive emotions and these emotions, in turn, affect literate language.

In friendship groups, expression of emotional terms was mediated by conflicts and resolutions. This was not the case for the non-friends groups. Following our predictions, it was probably the case that the general tenor of friendship elicited reflection upon emotions (as evidenced by emotional terms) after conflicts and resolutions. Following Dunn (1988), close relationships, like friendships, seem to support children's close attention to and reflection upon emotional processes.

Children's gender also affected expression of conflicts/resolutions and emotions differently in friend and non-friend conditions. Consistent with our hypothesized model, boys were high and girls were low on conflict/resolution in the friends conditions. The path from gender to conflicts/resolutions was not significant for the non-friend group. Girls, however, were high on expressed emotion in both conditions. The lack of gender differences for conflicts/resolutions between non-friends is consistent with Hartup's suggestion (Hartup, 1996; Hartup, et al., 1993) that conflictual talk is a manifestation of different relationships, for boys at least, not individual children.

Temperament had a direct effect on literate language for both groups. We suggest that the emotional intensity and activity characteristic of these children fostered an 'interactional' orientation toward peers and objects in their play environment. As noted by Hinde and colleagues (1985) active children tend to play interactively with peers. Slomkowski (1991) also found extraversion predicted children's expressive language. It is probably the case that active and emotionally intense children engage in varied sorts of social interaction with their peers. Children at this age typically engage in a particular form of interaction, pretend play, that supports literate language (Pellegrini and Galda, 1991). The contexts in which children were observed in this study encouraged children's pretend play and literate language.

It may be the case that temperamental differences of the sorts examined here might have negative effects on more traditional measures of literacy and school performance generally. Traditional assessments of literacy, as well as school literacy events, often are embedded in adult-rule-governed interactions which minimize peer interaction. In this regard, there would not be a good 'match' between this temperament and many classroom contexts. Such a regimen, we expect, would suppress children's exhibition of competence (Pellegrini and Horvat, 1995).

The effect of temperament on literate language, however, was mediated by conflicts and resolutions and emotional expression for both friends and non-friends. On the other hand, temperament had a direct effect on expression of emotion only for friends, not non-friends. Thus, temperament was supportive of the types of conflicts and resolutions leading to expression of emotion and reflection upon emotion, despite the social arrangement. Only the friendship condition, however, supported the expression of and reflection upon emotion, which led to literate language.

Conclusions/implications

In this chapter we examine only one dimension of temperament. It would be useful, with a larger sample, to chart the developmental trajectories of different sorts of children in close and diverse relationships.

It would be particularly useful if in the future researchers could test these process-related hypotheses within a longitudinal design. It would be especially interesting to see if the interactive styles which supported literate language for young children continued to predict literacy for older children. It may be the case that there is a closer match between the organizations of kindergarten classrooms, with their stress on movement and interaction, and the temperament of more active and sociable children. As children progress through the grades, the demand characteristics of classrooms change; they typically become more sedentary and less interactive places. It may be that these active and sociable children have a more difficult time in these classrooms than they did in the more open-ended classrooms.

Future research should also address the ways in which relevant aspects of friendship relate to both expression of emotion and other aspects of social understanding. For example, comparisons between 'best' friends and reciprocal friends are important. It should be the case that best friend, compared to friend, relationships are more supportive of cognitive reflection. At a more microanalytical level, examination of specific conflict and resolution styles is worthy. It may be the case that specific types of conflicts and resolutions maximize cognitive reflection. For example, conflicts around matters which friends consider relevant to their self definition (Tesser *et al.*, 1984) might foster, through self-comparison, cognitive reflection.

In Chapter 8 we will step back and look at children in more detail by examining case studies of first grade literacy learners as they interact in their classroom.

A case study of school-based literacy learning

> Children are scattered throughout the room with papers, pencils, books, and markers. Everyone is engaged in writing. There is a hum of talk as children ask, of those with whom they are sitting, how to spell words. Various children offer spellings and discuss which one is correct, the writer puts down what she considers the best, and then goes on. Children are murmuring to themselves, talking with Betty, the aide, and me [Lee]. Suddenly A bursts into song. Other children pick up her song and continue their writing, singing.
>
> (Fieldnotes, October 7 1992)

In just four weeks, the children in BS's first grade class have settled into the habits of literacy in their classroom. When they arrived in her room in late August many of them were not reading or writing, and did not see themselves as readers and writers. Within four weeks they were all so comfortable with themselves as literate people that they could write while singing. This chapter traces the refining of the development of literacy within the classroom community and then focuses on one child, beginning with his entry into first grade and ending near the culmination of his second grade year. We consider evidence of his literacy ability as indicated by samples of his reading and writing as it occurred naturally in the classrooms, and augmented by fieldnotes describing literacy events across the two years.

Here, as in other chapters, we define literacy as the ability to communicate through and about print. As children learn and develop, this ability becomes more elaborated, enabling them to read and write with greater fluency and control across a variety of texts and situations. Along with this, the *habit* of literacy also develops. This is evidenced by the joyful pursuit of literate skill and literacy opportunities.

Tracing literacy development in first and second grades

This study was conducted across two years by a team of university- and classroom-based researchers. During year 1 the team consisted of four: Lee Galda, Tony Pellegrini and Steve Stahl from the University of Georgia and the National Reading Research Center (NRRC), and Betty Shockley (BS) as both teacher-researcher and a member of the NRRC. The second year marked a shift in the research team, with Stahl not participating and Shockley moving full-time to the NRRC. The second grade classroom teacher did not participate as a research partner.

We began the study with a general question: what practices support literacy development in this particular whole-language classroom? As we participated in the life of the classroom we began to ask other, more specific questions, such as:

● How does the classroom teacher promote connections between home and school lives?
● How do the children make use of their home lives in the context of school?
● What is the role of oral language in the development of literacy?
● How does the classroom teacher promote a supportive, tightly knit literate community?
● How do the children support one another in literacy development?

During the second year of the study we continued to track the literacy development of six children, documenting the transition from first to second grade, and from a whole language classroom to a more skills-oriented classroom.

Methods

The design of this study was qualitative, a meta-case design that allowed a rich description of cases within cases. During year 1 the larger case was the classroom, and within that individual children were followed across the year. The class moved, almost completely intact, to second grade and the six children whose parents gave permission for them to continue in the study were followed during their second grade year; data from one of those six children are presented here. During the second year of data collection the children were the focal cases; the classroom was not studied as a unit, although it was observed as the context within which the focal children worked.

First grade

Classroom observations began on the second day of the school year when the university-based researchers visited the classrooms. By the second week, one of two university-based researchers observed each week. Data for this study consist of biweekly observations by the first author only. These observations continued biweekly through March, with one observation in April and a final observation in May. School ended the first week in June. The class was observed for full days at the beginning of the data collection, and then for the mornings, the time in which most of the literacy-related activities occurred. After a late lunch, the focus was on mathematics and free choice center time, during which time oral language samples were audiotaped once a month. As an observer-participant, Lee took extensive fieldnotes which were then transcribed and embedded with transcribed audio- and videotapes of literacy events.

The Home Literacy Journals were part of Betty's regular routine. Three times a week across the entire year the children took a book and their journal home where they read and responded to the book, using the journal, with others or independently. Additional home information came from the literacy network measure developed for this project that was adapted from the work of Cochran (Cochran and Riley, 1988). The questionnaire, which was administered by Betty during a parent–teacher conference in the spring, asked caregivers to identify the activities involving books, paper and pencils the child engaged in and with whom they did each. Information in the form of a HOME Inventory (Caldwell and Bradley, 1984) was gathered by Betty when she visited each of her students' homes during the spring quarter. (Psychometric information on these measures can be found in Chapter 5.)

Interviews were conducted in the fall, winter and spring by Lee and Betty. These interviews, in which both daily literacy events and broad beliefs and practices were discussed, were audiotaped and later transcribed. Other informal discussions during lunch or after school between Lee and Betty were noted in memos.

Individual student data for year 1 (as described in Chapter 5) also included a range of standardized literacy measures, informal literacy measures, audio- and videotapes of reading and writing events, classroom observations described in fieldnotes, literacy artifacts and Home Literacy Journals.

At the beginning, middle and end of first grade we administered the Stahl and Murray (1993) test of phonological awareness and Clay's

(1985) *Concepts about Print*. We also administered Clay's (1985) writing fluency measure, which asks children to write as many words as they can in 10 minutes, and a dictation measure which asks children to write a sentence from dictation. Informal literacy measures included a task in which children were asked to 'write a story about a dog and a cat', a timed writing sample also administered across the first grade year. Requests for children to read aloud from the trade books they had selected for independent reading were recorded. The children were also interviewed at the end of the year about their perceptions of themselves and others as literate persons.

Second grade

Data for year 2 consisted of formal and informal literacy measures, classroom observations, literacy artifacts, Home Literacy Journals and a single home visit by Betty in the spring. The case study children, along with the rest of their classmates, were tested at the beginning and end of the year by the school reading specialist, who used a standardized informal reading inventory. The children also read aloud a book of their choice and were again given the timed writing task at both the beginning and the end of the year. Oral language during center time was audiotaped once a month by a graduate assistant. Observations of the focal children in their classroom were made every two to three weeks by Lee through December, and then every two to three weeks by a graduate assistant through the end of April. Samples of students' writing were copied as were the Home Literacy Journals.

Data analysis

For this report, fieldnotes resulting from classroom observations were read and coded for significant themes and issues by both Betty, as the classroom teacher-researcher, and Lee, one of the participant observers. Following this, narrative descriptions of the first grade classroom were written and discussed by Betty and Lee. Then narrative descriptions of the behavior of the focal children were generated. Data from the literacy measures and the home information were then added to the narrative descriptions for a picture of individual children's literacy development across first and second grade.

The setting

Neighborhood School is a primary school for children aged 5–11 in Athens, GA, a medium-sized city in northeastern Georgia with a population consisting primarily of African Americans and Caucasians of varying economic situations. In the school 74 percent of the students were eligible for either free or reduced-fee lunch programs. The school is in a low to middle income, mixed race area. Some children walked or were driven to school; some rode the bus. The classrooms were roomy and class sizes small, with a maximum of twenty-two children in the first grade class and twenty-five in the second grade class. There was a full-time aide in first grade and a part-time aide in second.

The larger case: first grade

The school picture of Betty's classroom shows seventeen children (ten African American, one Asian, six Caucasian), one teacher and one teacher's aide, although there were as few as sixteen and as many as twenty-two students in the room at various times during the year. Two large desks, one for the aide and one for Betty, are close to the wall to the right of the door. They are piled with papers, a computer, newspapers, books, bookbags, coffee cups, signs, etc., all of the detritus of busy lives. They are also immediately out-of-view and forgotten once inside the door a few paces. Immediately to the front of the door is a listening center, and beyond that on the left-hand wall are shelves that hold toy bricks, puzzles, games and materials. There are four tables with six chairs each arranged on this side of the classroom. The back wall has a door leading outside and huge windows above a low cupboard which holds guinea pigs and a parakeet which often sings. The far right-hand wall is lined with bookshelves and hundreds of children's books. There's a large rug, some big pillows, and some stuffed animals nearby. A small stage area with boxes of books on the back is close to the front of the room, almost touching Betty's desk. There's an easel, a chart, a high stool and a tape recorder and mike at the edge of the stage. There are children's pictures, writing and other work everywhere – on bulletin boards and hanging from the ceiling. Several big books rest on the easel, a chart full of environmental sounds (like sirens) is tacked on the wall, and charts for jobs and sharing schedules hang from the cork strip above the chalkboard. There is plenty of space left for the children to sit on the floor in front of the stage.

Their teacher, Betty, had been teaching kindergarten and first grade for eleven years when the study began and was considered a master teacher, having received the teacher of the year award from her school and then school district, and being named the runner-up for teacher of the year in the state. She was, in both theory and practice, a whole language teacher who actively built a community of learners.

The *Oxford American Dictionary* defines community as '(1) a body of people living in one place . . . and considered as a whole; (2) a group with common interests or origins; and (3) fellowship'. A combination of all three meanings begins to describe Betty's class. They were indeed a community, people who lived and worked together inside and outside the walls of the classroom. The community building in Betty's classroom was a deliberate, planned act. In a discussion between Betty and Lee at the end of September, Lee asked Betty about the importance of community.

L: Community is always an underpinning for you, I would assume.
B: Right. It's just like family and maintaining family and marriage. You always have to work at it.
L: Yeah.
B: You know, it's never just a given. And so we learn to talk respectfully to each other, and we know that some people can have bad days and we're all human and we bring our outside life to this inside life, too, so that we can respect it and look at it and consider it. . . . The community building is just constant, but very aggressive in the beginning and consciously, I guess, . . . to make it very explicit that we are saying this because this is important to us because we live together and we need to know each other. . . . And with as much responsibility [in the classroom] as these children have, that community base has to be there. You can't say, 'Okay, y'all just go.' They've got to learn to share the books and make trade-offs and how to use their time.

(Interview, September 24)

The functioning of the community rested on the importance placed on oral sharing of the dailyness of children's lives, the students' freedom of choice and movement during independent reading, and the small group configuration and sea of talk (Britton, 1970) upon which reading and writing rested. As we noted in Chapters 6 and 7, children's friendships are an important dimension of classroom community.

At the beginning of the year Betty made explicit, deliberate comments that promoted self-efficacy. She helped the children feel that they were valued members of this community, realize that they could and should listen to and use each other's ideas and expertise, and understand how they could be responsible and thoughtful community members. As the year progressed, the connectedness of community members allowed them to work toward literacy in ways that each found useful and satisfying. What happened in this classroom was the kind of 'connected teaching' that rests on the view that every child has a unique perspective that is in some sense irrefutably 'right' by virtue of its existence. But the connected class transforms these private truths into 'objects' publicly available to the members of the class who, through 'stretching and sharing', add to themselves as knowers by individually absorbing their classmates' ideas. This connectedness rested on a very firm structure, with children knowing exactly what was expected of them and what their choices were.

B: [They need to know that] this time is for reading and this time is for writing and that means you have choices about what you write and what you read and what paper you use and where you sit and that kind of thing. But it doesn't mean you have the choice to go do legos or something.

(Interview, September 24)

Both individual choice and responsibility and social connectedness occurred within a predictable framework each day. Oral sharing time, writing workshop, reading workshop, whole class reading time and project centers time provided opportunities for children to make literate choices and to practice literacy in the company of literate others.

Oral sharing time

Oral sharing time had a special name, derived from a student's ritual opening during the previous school year. 'Y'All Know What?' became the call that beckoned students to an opportunity for literate talk that began each day. From the beginning children talked, listened and borrowed ideas from each other as they brought their lives to school and shared them orally. They told stories, explained toy brick constructions, planned their writing and retold familiar stories across the course of the year. Fieldnotes from September 1, during the second week of school, show the variety and excitement that permeated 'Y'All Know What?' and made it such a rich opportunity for literate talk.

It is first thing in the morning and 'Y'All Know What?' time has just begun. Jason shows and talks about his penny that was squished on a railroad track; Ami shows the story she wrote the day before, holding the book up for the class to see and moving it around the circle. She comments: 'I was gonna write "the end" but I didn't find out the words.' Kimberly sounds out 't h e e n d' and Betty says, 'I'll help you.' Ami ends with, 'But I didn't have time to write it.' Jenna tells a story about the sea and Betty comments, 'Oh, Jenna, you ought to write about that sometime.' Jenay says she's going to have a party and puts a sign-up sheet on Betty's desk. Penjata tells an elaborate story full of 'and thens' and punctuated by the refrain, 'Where's my bookbag?' uttered in a very dramatic voice. Betty chimes in, 'You know what? It's neat to write stories with characters talking like that, like you really talk.' Rick then tells his story, with sound effects, about swimming in a neighbor's pool – a very exaggerated, funny story. Betty says, 'Oh, what a tall tale that is!' She then turns to the group and asks, 'Why do you like Rick's story?' Various children respond, 'Because it was funny.' Betty says, 'Yes. And he used sound effects.' Jenay comments, 'And he said "hey, man".' Betty notes, 'Yes, he talked like people would. So that you can understand it. Rick took something that really happened to him, like he really went swimming, and put extra stuff in it and made it fun. I loved it. I loved everybody's stories. It was so fun to hear what you have to say. You're all so interesting.'

Already, just one week after school has begun, the children have begun to display a personal style, relate oral language to their writing, and borrow ideas, language and structures from each other. These things originated with the children, but Betty made them explicit, helping the children see what they already knew how to do.

As the children changed and the classroom community developed, 'Y'All Know What?' evolved over time from a forum for sharing home lives with school companions and for rehearsing potential ideas for writing to a time to retell familiar stories, demonstrating to all the skill of the storyteller and engaging the audience in a happy recreation of a familiar tale. As the children became comfortable with sharing oral stories from home, Betty introduced them to new possibilities during sharing time, just as she moved from asking everyone to share each day to having smaller numbers of children sharing on assigned days. Rick's introduction of the tall tale on September 1 provided an early

introduction to the many possibilities for oral sharing that were present in Betty's room. After this day children continued to recount things
that happened at home and to describe how they wrote stories or built
toy brick creations in the classroom, but they also began to make up
stories, tall tales that often found their way into the writing workshop.
As the children became increasingly familiar with the stories in the
many tradebooks in Betty's classroom, they developed favorites, stories that they enjoyed retelling. Thus another option for sharing time
began. As the children retold familiar stories they made the language
of the story their own, adopting the words, rhythms and intonations of
the written word as they sought to re-create familiar tales. These occasions were always highly interactive, with the whole class listening
carefully and helping the teller remember sequence, phrasing, intonation and tone. Jenna attempted to retell *The Three Billy Goats Gruff*
after Betty read it to the whole class:

> Once upon a time there was three goats. Three billy goat Gruffs
> and they were brothers. They wanted to go in the meadow because
> they wanted to get fat. Then they were walking the hillside they
> saw a BIGGGG bridge (indicates the bridge with a gesture) and
> there was a troll, a little troll who lived under the bridge. . . . And
> when the first . . . the real small billy goat walked across the bridge
> . . . the troll came out and said . . . Trit trot, trit, trot . . . and then
> the troll came out . . . and he said, 'Who is [Another student: Who
> is that jumping on my bridge?] that trapping on my bridge?' . . .
> And the little billy goat said, 'Oh, it's only I, the little billy goat.'
> . . . and then he said 'I will gobble you up.' [Another student
> echoes: 'I will gobble you up.']

Toward the end of the telling, the other students were enrapt in Jenna's
re-creation. Just as the big billy goat is telling the troll to 'Come on
out here and see what you can do', another student chimes in: 'Come
on out here and see what you could do. Hit him with a big horn!' Not
only the storyteller was making the story language her own.

In whatever form it took, oral sharing time was an invaluable opportunity for students to use language to share their lives in school and
out, and to explore ideas and experiences as readers and writers.

Writing workshop

During writing workshop the children worked individually and col-
laboratively on writing projects of their choice for 30–40 minutes.

Never was the workshop quiet; rarely was the talk off task. Working at small tables promoted collaboration among the children whether Betty or her aide were there or not. The description of writing workshop at the beginning of this chapter describes the feeling in the room: writing workshop was always filled with the hum of busy voices, if not song.

Many of the children composed aloud as they wrote, either saying the words that they intended to put on paper or spelling aloud. An audible vocalization when spelling meant immediate help from neighbors, even if not explicitly asked for. On September 30 John is reading his story to Lee, who is seated at the table with him and four other children, when Jason offers unsolicited help:

John: (Leaning over his paper) One time/
Jason: (Leaning over John's paper) One starts with an O.
Lee: Jason says that one starts with an O.
Jason: 'Cause I remember from kindergarten.

Help with spelling came in a variety of forms, as Kimberly demonstrated on September 1. When Shuntae asks the table at large, 'How do you spell Ms. Shockley?' Kimberly jumps up and gets a book, returning with it open to the inside page, saying, 'Here's how to spell Shockley. Just go get a book that her name is on and copy it. Her name is on all of the books in the classroom.'

Collaborating during writing also involved talk to plan writing with a writing partner. Jenna and Brooke often worked together, with both planning the writing, Jenna doing the actual writing, and Brooke illustrating the piece. At other times they would work on parallel books, with each writing on separate papers but making sure that they were writing the same thing. At other times, especially toward the end of the year, they would sit together, offering each other help with spelling, with ideas, and being a 'listening ear' when asked, but working on totally separate pieces.

There were many varied opportunities for talk during writing workshop, and the children had both informal opportunities to move around the room as well as structured opportunities to work with new people when they worked with different groups. Never told to write silently, they used talk to support their language learning as they took chances and grew as writers.

Time to share writing grew from a time for children to show each other what they had done that day to a time for children to show their work and invite helpful feedback from their classmates. As individual students read their writing, Betty and other students would comment on their drawings, the words they chose to use, the punctuation they used and the general nature of their piece. Ranging from 'Oh, I like that part' to 'That's funny!' student comments indicated that they were attending to the author's voice and took their role of audience seriously, just as they did when they were at their tables during writing workshop.

Reading workshop

Reading workshop, when children were free to select books, read and respond as they chose, followed writing workshop for most of the school year and began as children finished writing or sharing their writing and moved toward the hundreds of books that were in their classroom. As children selected their books they moved to wherever they were comfortable reading. Some returned to the tables where they had been writing. Some sprawled on the rug near the bookshelves, others sat on the stage in the center front of the room or in front of the adult desks which were over in a corner. Some took books to the audiocenter and listened to them on tape. A few students would go out into the hall for a quiet spot. Jenay liked best to get into a carton that served as a 'covered wagon' for the study of the 'old days' during center time, that was near the reading corner, taking all of the stuffed animals with her, and read to them. Children read individually, in pairs, or in groups of three. Some worked with Betty and her aide, some read to whoever was observing that day.

The fieldnotes from October 27 illustrate some of the variety of partnerships and configurations that were possible during reading workshop:

> Children move into reading time gradually. Ivy points as she reads. She's using picture cues for the nouns. Adrienne sits next to her, reading the pictures and telling the story from memory, running her fingers over the words. Ivy insists on helping. Pakaysanh is looking at a dinosaur pop-up book, *David Dreams of Dinosaurs*. John asks me to read *Berenstain Bear's Trick or Treat*. A group of children are gathered around Betty, reading. Ami is still working on her drawing. Pakaysanh gets *The Magic School Bus*. Some children are in the hall reading and putting a play together. Jason reads from memory, looking at words only when he needs

prompting. Marianesha and Adrienne are partner reading *Rosie's Walk*. Dennis, Andrew, Desmond, Jenay, Ivy, Jenna, and Jason are now in the hall reenacting *Rosie's Walk* with cards.

(Fieldnotes, October 27)

As with writing time, there was a lot of helping talk. Children chatted quietly about the books they were selecting, often arranging to swap after they had finished with their first choices. Sometimes children would take the pile of books written by the author the class was studying and a small group would work their way through the pile. The students knew who was a good reader and who could help them when they ran into difficulties. It was common to hear children asking those around them for help decoding difficult words, sharing funny bits from the text, and doing partner reading, alternating pages or characters' dialogue.

Whole class reading

Whole class reading looked different each day, but there was always the opportunity for oral interaction around the texts being read. Sometimes Betty read a big book, inviting children to look closely at the words and the pictures. When this happened, the talk was concerned with sounds of letters, words, placement, linearity, illustration – text match and information in the illustrations. At other times Betty read from regular trade books and the talk revolved around the author and the story. Children would readily discuss the choices the author made in telling the story, other books that they remembered as they related to the story, and things that had occurred in their lives that related to the story. In this respect Betty's classroom looked like others where children listen and respond to trade books (Cochran-Smith, 1984).

Because Betty valued oral language experiences so much, the whole class reading time frequently moved into dramatic re-enactments; these gave children an opportunity to use talk to plan, to perform and to respond. Further, like the oral retelling of familiar stories, dramatic re-enactments provided the opportunity for children to make book language their own.

On a day when Betty read *The Three Billy Goats Gruff* during whole class reading, the children asked to do a play. The following dialogue is taken from a video/audiotape and fieldnotes for March 2.

Betty: You all are asking me if maybe we could do a play of *Billy Goats Gruff*. Now to talk about that. Let's see. Well, let me ask, Dennis, how many characters do we need?

Students: Four.

Betty: Oh, boy! There are a lot of Dennises here. You all think fast. Four characters. Who might they be?

Students: Troll and three goats.

Betty: The troll and three goats.

Student: Somebody needs to be the bridge.

[Students are all talking at once, when one takes a bench that is in the reading corner and begins to drag it into the center of the room.]

Betty: Oh, that's a good bridge.

[Students and Betty discuss who will play which parts, that there will be several groups of players, and that those not performing will be the audience.]

Betty: Hey, that looks like a meadow. Now, see. Why don't you pretend that that rug is the grass and you can come from this side.

Jenay: Can I be the narrator?

This was just one of many times when these students played with the stories they were reading. Since music was so prevalent in this classroom they often turned their stories into 'operas', singing, for example, Sendak's *Chicken Soup with Rice* and *Pierre*. Don and Audrey Wood's *The Napping House* and *King Bidgood's in the Bathtub* were also dramatized, providing real opportunities to use story language and structure. These dramatic re-enactments did not take place only during or after reading. They also found their way into project centers at the end of the day.

Project centers

Children were free to choose from a number of centers at the end of the day. What these centers were and how they worked was negotiated between Betty and her students, providing yet another opportunity to use oral language in a meaningful way. Many students chose to work on the writing that they had begun earlier in the day; others chose to read. Some played with bricks or did puzzles or went to special centers that related to the science, social studies or math curriculum. Many chose to do plays, re-enacting stories that they had heard or read together. These performances sometimes took place in the hall, where a dramatic play center was set up and shared by the other primary grade classrooms in the wing. This center housed kitchen equipment, tables and chairs, and a big box of dress-up clothes. Often, small groups of children would organize a play during centers time, playing to an audience of themselves usually, but sometimes performing for the rest of the class just before dismissal. Children would do re-enactments in the classroom, also, working on the small stage in the center front of the room.

Children also used this time to do dramatic readings of favorite stories with a peer or peers, perching on a high stool or standing on the stage. It was obvious that these readings, like the re-enactments, were done primarily for the readers' pleasure, rather than audience reaction.

Beyond the classroom

Betty also encouraged reading and writing at home with Home Literacy Journals. Students took home a book and their journal three times a week to read, talk and respond with someone at home. Talk was encouraged, with Betty often reminding students that 'Talk is the most important thing.' Children were free to work with anyone at home, and there was great variety. The journals also gave Betty the opportunity to carry on literate discussions in writing with her students and their families. The home journal procedure is more fully described in *Engaging Families* (Shockley *et al.*, 1995).

Echoing Calkins's (1991: 7) description of writing, Betty believed that 'Literacy is lifework, not deskwork.' This meant that students in this class brought their lives to school through story, both oral and written, and spent much of their time in school and outside of school negotiating meaning through language. Children's literature also provided a significant and dependable bridge supporting literate connections between home and school (Shockley *et al.*, 1995). Books as well as written and oral stories of home and school life passed through both school and home settings daily and purposefully.

The teacher's role

The community that Betty and her students built was rich with talk, thanks to Betty's planning and her belief in the importance of talk (Galda *et al.*, 1996). During an interview on January 14, Lee and Betty discussed the ways in which Betty deliberately built a classroom community that supported children's acquisition of literacy, considering the role that Betty played as a literate other in that classroom community.

Betty: Because of my personal connectedness [to reading and writing] I have become a more skillful leader of literate wisdom for my students. I've been there, I am there, I'll always be there . . .

Lee: You know, I think when you and Barbara [another teacher] say things like you 'just try to get out of the kids' way,' you really mean it and it is true. You get out of the kids' way because you know that you have given them a variety of ways, ideas for the paths that they can take, for the ways that they can go, for the books that they can read, for the people they can read with, for the strategies they can use [for reading], for the strategies they can write with, for the ideas they can use. They all have lots of choices that they can make, but not choices that they thought up all by themselves. . . . So when you get out of their way you get out of their way to allow them to do things that either you have told them about or things that they have discovered with your help [and that of their friends and family]. It's not like you are sitting saying, 'Okay kids, become literate.' When I watch you, I think you do an amazing amount of teaching. You're always connecting things for kids, connecting books to books. Today Rick said 'Kaboom' and you said, 'No, Anansi isn't here, but that would be a good one.' That's something literate people do. You did it, it was no big deal, no fuss. They all [make those connections] now because you have been doing that since day one.

Betty: It was wonderful to watch.

Lee: So you get out of their way, but you also behave like a literate person and demonstrate a lot of literate behaviors and often will make it explicit. . . . You get out of their way to let them pursue literacy in their own manner, but you give them tools, you give them strategies, you really do.

Betty did, indeed, get out of the children's way, but only after she was sure that they knew that there are ways to go, that she was 'helping them to get on their way' (interview, January 24) to literacy.

On their way to literacy: John's journey

What happened in Betty's classroom was a communal experience as engaged in by individual members of that community. By looking closely at the literacy growth of one of these children, John, we can begin to understand how individual children made use of the opportunities that Betty and their family provided for them, and how that did or did not continue to sustain them during their second grade year.

John's story

On entry into first grade John described himself in words and pictures. He lived with both parents and his older sister; both parents were professionals. In answering a questionnaire about himself and his interests, he indicated that he liked to read Marc Brown's *Arthur* books, owned 134 books, liked comics better than books, enjoyed the *National Geographic* and felt that *Ninja Turtles* was the best book he had ever read. He watched fewer than one movie a week, and only one television show per day.

John at home

John's home environment was so rich and varied that it met the criteria for 57 of the 59 descriptors on the HOME Inventory. Many varied stimulating experiences were available to John, including a trip to the Smithsonian, access to books and sports and musical experiences. His parents provided a safe, pleasant and stable life in which John was supported in his emotional, social, physical, cognitive and linguistic development.

His mother wrote a description of John at the beginning of the year:

> John is a very sweet child although at times he is slightly mischievous. He has a tremendous mechanical aptitude. Give him something to build and he can be enthralled for hours. When he is interested in something, he has practically endless concentration. If he's bored, he flits from activity to activity. John loves to be read to. He can recognize some words and is just about ready to read. He also seems to do well with numbers. He can do simple subtraction when it is explained in concrete terms. When he was three, he began riding a two-wheeled bike. He has good coordination. Just before he broke his arm, he had learned to do both

the backstroke and breaststroke by watching swimmers on television. He just jumped in the pool and started doing the strokes! Ask him about our Fourth of July trip to Washington, D. C. He loved the city and the various monuments. John loves [toy bricks]. If you use [toy bricks], I'm convinced he can learn anything. You'll find that he has a quick, funny wit. Sometimes it's a little too quick. Sometimes he's sleepy and grumpy in the mornings. Sometimes he becomes shy and embarrassed. I suppose all in all, he's a fairly well adjusted boy, ready to have fun and I hope ready to learn in first grade.

John at school

John was ready to learn in first grade, and quickly found friends and a working routine that was comfortable for him. The literacy measures given at the beginning of the year indicated that John had a basic understanding of how print works, and was just beginning to read decontextualized text. He knew that print rather than pictures carried the message in a text, was comfortable with directionality when reading, understood beginning and end, could recognize inversions, and understood the concept of letters, but did not indicate an understanding of basic punctuation or word or letter sequence within words. He wrote four words when asked to write as many words as he knew.

The informal reading inventory indicated frustration at reading the level 1 preprimer, *Bells*, when presented to him as a typescript lacking in illustrations, although John did select and look at trade books in the classroom and at home with obvious pleasure. He could distinguish some beginning and ending consonant sounds, as well as a few medial vowels.

Except for the title and the formula ending, he used only pictures to convey his story. By the end of January, when the second story was produced, he was relying on words alone to convey his meaning. Many of his letters are backward, there is little attention to spacing, and there is no consistent use of upper and lower case letters. His invented spelling was frequently unreadable by Betty, and sometimes even John could not decode what he had written. His 45-word story included a title, a problem, action, past tense, and both a happy and a formulaic ending, demonstrating his tacit knowledge of the story genre.

By the end of May, John was spelling more words conventionally and was reliably putting spaces between his words. His 73-word story, still with a title and a formulaic ending, was in the past tense. This story contains an introduction (one day), a problem, actions and a resolution. There are also character relationships, emotion and time markers.

At the end of that first year John wrote 40 words when asked to write all the words that he knew in 10 minutes. He was reading at a first grade level fluently (as measured by the informal reading inventory) and could read the trade books, *The Gunnywolf* and 'A Lost Button' from Lobel's *Frog and Toad*, fluently. His end of the year questionnaire indicated that John liked to read and write and considered himself a competent reader and writer. When asked, 'Are you a writer?' John responded with a grin that lit up his face and a resounding 'yes'. His advice for helping someone learn to read was direct: 'Look at the picture close and look at the first letter.' For writing he would say to do what his mother told him to do: 'Write my abcd's and then try it.'

In response to a parent questionnaire sent home by Betty at the end of the year, John's mother wrote the following:

Can your child read? Yes, he can read simple books.

Does your child like to read? Yes, he gets a sense of fulfillment and accomplishment from reading.

Does your child choose to read? Yes, although he wants the reassurance of someone there to help 'just in case'.

How do you think your child learned to read? John learned to read first by recognizing words. Lately he has begun sounding out parts of unfamiliar words.

Does your child like to write? He loves to write and invents wonderful stories.

Please tell me about your child now that he has finished first grade. John has had a wonderful year. He has loved learning and feels that he can accomplish anything. It has been great seeing his self-confidence grow as he became more and more successful. Thank you for recognizing John's own special brand of giftedness. . . . I hope that [the principal] will keep the class together as they move to second grade in order to continue allowing the children to experience the very special kind of learning they have participated in this year. . . . I congratulate everyone who has been a part of John's learning this year, for a job well done. If we can keep him this excited year after year we will have a truly motivated learner! He's off to a great start!

John discovers how written language works

It is September 30, the sixth week of school, and the children have just come in from recess. They gather on the rug to sing 'Hambone' and then move to the tables for writing workshop. John is sitting at a table with Dennis, Adrienne, Ami and Jason. He's concentrating on the paper in front of him, adding letters to the words that he's scattered around the page.

Lee: Hi, John. What are you doing?
John: I'm trying to fill some letters.
Lee: Trying to fill some letters in?
John: Writing right there.

John reads his message to himself. The words are scattered around the page and he is attempting to match his message to the words he's written. He erases BIK (bike) to write SNAK (snake) and tries again.

OWNT TIM RTN MY

MY RIN MY BIK MY

SEE BIK SNAK

He reads: 'One time I was riding my bike and I saw a snake.' He continues to work, stopping to ask:

John: How do you spell riding?
Lee: How do you spell riding? What does Ms. Shockley tell you to do when you need to know how to spell something? Sound it out?
Betty: I usually say, 'What's that first sound you hear? What's that last sound you hear?'
Lee: What's the first sound you hear in riding?
Betty: What's the next sound you hear, maybe?
John: I.
Lee: Rrriiiddd. . . .
Jason: See, the word ride is in the word.

Lee: Okay, John. ri . . . ding.
John: Ri . . . T?

John continues to work on his story until it comes closer to what he wants it to say.

John: I can read this all by myself!
Lee: Well, read it to me, John. I'd love to hear it.
John: One time when I was riding my bike, I saw a snake.
Lee: One time when I was riding my bike, I saw a snake. And there's a picture of you riding your bike and seeing a snake! That's wonderful!
John: I need to write A. I need to write I, there. [Does it.] There. And another I here. [Does so.] One time when I was riding my bike, I saw . . .
Lee: Can you read it to me now, John?
John: I have to write 'my'.
Lee: You have to write 'my'? Now can you read it to me?
John: Where should I put 'the' in here? I have to put 'the' in here.

After some discussion with others, John asks Lee to read.

Lee: One time I ride. . . .
John: I need 'was'.
Lee: What do you need there?
John: Was.
Lee: Was?
John: Right there.
Lee: So you're going to erase ride and put was there?
John: Mmmm, yeah. And erase 'bike' and that [points] and. . . . And then I'll put 'was' there and then that over here.

John continues restating his message and erasing words on his page until they are in the order in which he is saying them:

OWN TIM WN I WS RITN MY BIK I SEE A SNAK.

Quite satisfied with his success, he went to sharing time ready to read his story to his friends.

This episode illustrates the perseverance with which John approached literacy learning during this first grade year. It also high-lights the importance of time, choice, community and good faith, or positive expectations, that supports the evolution of such breakthrough moments. John had time to work through this complex process of realigning written words with spoken language. He knew this time would be available to him every day and day-upon-day he added to his literate knowledge base, sometimes in big ways and sometimes by taking it one step at a time. Choice of topic and the consistent support of his friends also contributed to John's level of investment in coming to understand the writing process.

Undergirding these transactions, however, is the good faith John had in himself as a competent learner and the good faith of his family and teacher. John had observed print written and read in a linear left-to-right manner in many contexts. His parents read to him often at home. In school his teacher had modeled such reading behaviors by pointing out the words while reading big books and little books to John individually and to the whole class. When John recognized the inconsistencies between what he wanted to say and what he had actually written, these prior experiences with print had a meaningful effect: he figured out how written language works. Until he puzzled out the conventions for himself, the examples in his world of print remained outside his level of application.

John was so persistent because he had the opportunity and support to be so. He worked quietly and diligently throughout the year in the company of his peers and both accepted and gave help graciously, a full participant in classroom life in the first grade.

John as a second grader

John's home life remained stable as he moved into the second grade and made the transition to a new classroom life. Many of his classmates moved with him, so he was in the company of peers with whom he was comfortable reading and writing. His second grade teacher, Ms. X, continued the practice of Home Literacy Journals at the beginning of the year, although only once as opposed to three times a week. Likewise, reading and writing workshops were in place in second grade, but the time spent in reading and writing decreased while the time spent in whole class instruction (such as whole class reading and mini-lessons in writing) increased. This classroom was a skills oriented classroom with certain practices, like reading and writing workshop, incorporated and adapted from whole language approaches. However, the context surrounding these workshops was fundamentally different from the first grade context where a whole language philosophy clearly guided practice. Although the children could and did talk to each other during writing workshop, there was little collaboration other than help with spelling, and there was very little talk during reading workshop. The children worked primarily separately rather than jointly.

Beginning in the middle of his first grade year and continuing throughout this year, John was out of the classroom each morning during independent reading time when he participated in the gifted program.

John began the year about where he ended his first grade year. His informal reading inventory indicated a first grade instructional level and he read 'A Lost Button' from *Frog and Toad* fluently as well; his comprehension was excellent in both cases. By the end of second grade John was reading at a second grade instructional level, but the comment on the informal reading inventory echoed the comment from the fall: John read slowly, hesitantly, and with a notable lack of confidence. He did, however, read the trade book, Stevens's *The Tortoise and the Hare,* fluently and with expression.

Although John wrote less often than he had done in first grade, his writing ability did continue to develop. The first 'cat and dog' story that he wrote in second grade was composed on October 22. This 68-word story begins in the middle of the action with the chase, focuses on the action in the apple tree as the cat attempts to keep away from the dog, and ends with a resolution of the problem and a conclusion, as well as a formulaic ending. His writing is an interesting mixture of conventional and invented spelling, with some of the invented spellings very difficult to decode. He is consistent in selecting an appropriate initial consonant sound, uses vowels as placeholders, uses long vowel sounds appropriately, and hears syllables within longer words. At the end of second grade John wrote a 69-word story containing a beginning, a problem, action and an abrupt, formulaic ending. His spelling is generally conventional and entirely readable. He uses only two periods in the whole story, not counting the one at the end of his title.

In John's writing workshop folder there are several pieces, each one limited to a page or less and usually done in one sitting. There was no extended writing across time, no book production, and, seemingly, little emotional investment. A good student, John did his work quietly and well. This time, when asked at the end of the year, 'Are you a writer?' he didn't smile, but he still said 'yes'.

John as a learner

It seems to us that after two years of learning with and about John, we need to acknowledge again the insights his parents offered in the very beginning of our study. For instance, they knew that John's strengths included 'a tremendous mechanical aptitude. Give him something to build and he can be enthralled for hours.' We wonder if supporting John's process of 'building' his concepts of written language one word at a time as in our writing workshop example could be a reason for his high level of perseverance? As a cautionary note, his parents want us to also know that 'sometimes [he] becomes shy and embarrassed'. Should we keep this information in mind when we characterize John's oral reading in an evaluative context as 'slow' and 'hesitant' with 'a notable lack of confidence'? Does he read more fluently when in a more comfortable setting such as with his family or peers? Yes, he does. And, could the information that 'he learned to do the backstroke and breaststroke by watching swimmers on television' speak to us of the importance of students having many opportunities to be aware of the literate next steps of their peers? How wonderful when we remember the times our students seemingly did as John did, 'just jump in the pool and start doing the strokes'!

Could not John's family be describing many children and not just their son when they write, 'When he is interested in something, he has practically endless concentration. If he's bored, he flits from activity to activity'? And, if such conditions of engagement – that is learning by doing, attention to areas of interest, time to immerse oneself in particular areas of study, and a sense of shared community – are claimed by teachers, parents and students, could we prepare for some very joyful noise?

Untold stories

There were, of course, other children in the classroom with John, and these children have their own particular stories, in spite of the similarities they share with John. Rick, fluent and precocious in his oral storytelling, learned to read and write and work with others during his first grade year only to have a difficult second grade experience that culminated in special placement. And there was Desmond, a quiet, African American with a tough exterior that didn't quite mask the sweet boy inside, who was supported and encouraged at home and in school as a first grader, and who learned to read and write, and accept and give help. He became increasingly withdrawn and angry during his second grade year, choosing not to read and write even during class time.

But there was also Jenna, a bright and friendly child, who flowered in the atmosphere of her first grade classroom despite the recent death of her mother, and continued to grow and learn throughout second grade, moving into reading chapter books like the *Little House* series and producing stories and expository pieces of increasing complexity. Adrienne, a shy African American girl, also continued to quietly work at becoming literate, progressing from a child who was not comfortable nor fluent in reading and writing, to a competent user of written language by the end of her first grade year.

Each of these children and their classmates made what they could of their school and home experiences. For some, the congruence between home and school, the opportunities at home and at school, and their particular strengths and needs provided the context they needed as they developed as literate people. Others got lost along the way.

Conclusion

What practices supported literacy development in this particular whole-language classroom? The deliberate valuing of children's lives at home, the connection between home and school via a literacy task, and the establishment of a social, supportive literate community were key to the functioning of Betty's classroom. Oral sharing time, writing and reading workshops, whole class reading and project centers were rich contexts that supported the children as they developed their ability to communicate through and about print and cultivated the habit of literacy. Each of these contexts contained talk – talk about language, talk about the children's lives – that enriched and, indeed, enabled the children's learning. Collectively and individually, these children learned literacy through exploratory and explanatory talk with their peers as well as instruction from their teacher.

While some of the structures of classroom life, such as journals, reading workshop and writing workshop, were present in both the first and the second grade classrooms, the oral interaction surrounding literacy events and the explicit valuing of home experiences decreased substantially in second grade. Without oral interaction, reading and writing became individual when Rick and Desmond still needed the collaborative support of their peers. Jenna, Adrienne and John did continue to progress in their literacy development, but without the rich resource of their peers.

Perhaps the most important factor in the complexity of the literacy experiences reported here was the teacher. Betty believed in the worth of each child and in the worth of oral collaboration. She was gifted enough to put these beliefs into practice in ways that created multiple opportunities for children to support each other as they learned to read and write. And they did.

Chapter 9

What is to be done?

This book has been about a research program into ways in which children learn to read and write in schools. Our work has followed a developmental psychological approach to studying children in different contexts. The results and discussion have, we hope, made a contribution to the further understanding of children's development.

Like other types of field-based research the distinction in our work between applied and basic research is blurred, if such a distinction is of any use at all. In field research, particularly research conducted in schools, understanding the ways in which children learn is, we think, simultaneously applied and basic. We suggest that 'basic' issues in learning and development cannot be understood without examining the 'applied' processes of learning in schools. It is necessary to study schooling in order to understand the ways in which children learn to read and write school-based texts.

It follows from our recommendation to minimize the distinctions between applied and basic research, that the implications of this research should be viewed as testable ideas. That is, we present ideas on the ways in which children can be taught to use literate language and to read and write. The degree to which these recommendations are efficacious is an empirical question which should be tested by teachers and researchers. This sort of empirical basis for educational practice should, in turn, guide policy on teaching and schooling.

In this chapter we discuss implications of our research for teaching children in schools. These implications come directly from our research and address issues related to adult–child book reading and interaction, as well as peer interaction in literacy events. As we have demonstrated above, children, as they are read to by parents, are systematically exposed to and 'taught' literate language. Children then take this register and use it with their peers, first in pretend play, and then later in more realistic peer discourse.

Joint reading between children and adults

Being read to is one of the more robust predictors of children's success in school, generally, and in school-based literacy instruction, more generally. Of course being read to is confounded with social economic status to the degree that poor children, generally, have far fewer books in their homes relative to middle class children. That these same books and their corresponding design features are also similar to the literacy materials in much of school-based literacy lessons merely reinforces this divide between poor children and their middle class counterparts.

In this chapter we center our recommendations on adults reading to children with limited experiences with books typically used in schools. This generally means children of poverty, or children 'at-risk' for school failure. We concentrate on this group simply because they have a more difficult time with school-based literacy instructions than their middle class counterparts.

We view our task here as providing children with the opportunities to learn the register of school-based literacy. Access to this register also provides access to otherwise unavailable sources of power.

There have typically been two solutions to the problem of poor children's failure in school literacy. The first, and more traditional, solution has been to change the nature of children's home environments. The assumptions here are that children fail because of something they lack, whether it be the unavailability of trade books in the home or a mother not reading those books to them.

Generally, homes of poor children are not thought of as 'literate environments' in the same way as middle class homes. *Literate environment* usually means children and others interacting around a variety of print forms, including trade books, typically of the sort also used in school-based literacy events. The literacy event, *par excellence*, of course, is the joint book reading context of child and parent (Heath, 1982; Teale, 1984). As we have shown earlier, through interactions around trade books children come to learn the rules of school-based literacy events, e.g. being able to label aspects of familiar texts (Heath, 1989). Recommendations for reduction of 'risk' for failure in school-based literacy typically include exposing mothers and children to trade books as well as school-like interaction styles around the books, such as labeling pictures and labeling letters (e.g. Whitehurst *et al.*, 1988).

In short, something is seen as wrong or deficient with the ways in which mothers socialize their children and remediation of these patterns is recommended. Recommended remediation strategies are those which typify middle class joint book reading events involving mothers and children. School literacy events, in this model, reflect the values of mainstream culture and, consequently, strive toward cultural homogeneity.

The second solution to the problem of poor children's failure in school-based literacy assumes that the locus of risk resides in the school, not the family and child. Though less common than the first and dominant model of failure, this solution assumes that children fail in school-based literacy because of the content and organization of schools, curriculum and of the interactional styles of teachers. Members of this group argue that schools, by their very nature, sort children. Risk can be reduced, according to this model, by incorporating home-based literacy events into the school curriculum. Unlike the first model, cultural heterogeneity, not homogeneity, is a goal of this approach.

We propose a third solution, one which considers school-based language and literacy as one specific register, among many others, that children should learn. Blame is not assessed; we merely assume that there are different rules for speech and literacy events in different speech communities. Home and school are two such communities and children should have access to both.

School language and literacy, like home language and home literacy, are examples of linguistic variation. High or low status is not assigned to either. We do recognize, however, that the different registers yield differential access to power; thus children should be taught the register that can help them gain access to power (Delpit, 1990).

Cazden (1970) made a similar point in addressing the Black English difference/deficit debate by noting that the situations in which language users are placed determine the form of language that will be used. Because different contexts have different rules for language use, language users appear more or less competent as a function of their knowledge of the rules of different contexts. That language and other forms of behavior typically vary as a function of context, presents a need to understand the rules that correspond to specific context if we hope to understand the reasons why certain children succeed and fail in school. This argument is like the language-game metaphor. Differential performance is merely a reflection of differential knowledge of specific contexts.

Also following Cazden's (1970) argument, definitions of linguistic competence and literacy need to be re-examined. While literacy curricula have been critiqued for not reflecting our knowledge of children and language, it is also known that the curricula for non-mainstream children are even more problematical (Au and Kawakami, 1984;

Delpit, 1990). For example, the standard materials used in literacy events with non-mainstream culture often do not motivate children to participate (Au and Kawakami, 1984). Current research suggests that curricula should move from the formal or structural to the functional. Literacy, in this tradition, would be defined as participants in a literacy event sharing knowledge from different sources; participating in joint activities around written text; and trading roles and skills in reading, writing and speaking (Heath, 1989).

Our work with non-mainstream culture African American mothers and their Head Start children in the southeastern United States showed how mothers' and children's exhibition of competence in a literacy event was influenced by features of the texts read. Our initial work with a similar group of mothers and children showed that their interactions around traditional children's books, i.e. trade books, was consistent with the research literature cited above; that is, neither mother nor child exhibited the interaction strategies characteristic of school-based literacy.

The interesting question then became: why? This caused us to step back and examine the ways in which texts generally affected interaction styles, the types of text that were familiar to these families, and the ways in which they differed from the trade books used in mainstream culture homes.

Isolated bits of research provided some guidance by suggesting genre differences in books read to children (e.g. Cornell *et al.*, 1988; Pellegrini *et al.*, 1990; Sulzby and Teale, 1987); for example, when adults read narratives (or stories) to children, generally, little interpersonal interaction is observed; expository texts (e.g. labeling books such as alphabet books) elicit much interaction. When our mothers and children were exposed to both traditional narrative and expository texts we found that the texts did indeed elicit different types of interaction styles. With the latter, mothers and children both exhibited more and more varied interaction. There was very little interaction around narrative texts. The reason for this seems relatively simple: narrative texts are unified by an explicit theme which is sufficient to sustain children's attention to the text. Indeed, children often protest when overly zealous parents interrupt narratives to ask school-like questions of their children.

Expository texts, on the other hand, are not explicitly unified by a theme. Instead, we typically have a series of isolated pictures. Again, the alphabet book is illustrative of the genre. *C is for car and d is for dog*. This format invites interaction. Middle class mothers typically ask children to label the pictures and children often relate the pictures to outside experiences. Culturally different families exhibit these strategies but only when they were interacting around text presented in a more familiar format (Pellegrini *et al.*, 1990).

To choose familiar texts we must know about the texts that are present in different communities. We need to understand diverse literacy events if we are to design school curricula which maximize the likelihood of non-mainstream culture children's success. Most non-mainstream culture families, like those described by Heath (1983) and ourselves, do not have children's books in the home. Many families do, however, receive and interact around a local newspaper and/or sales flyers sent through the mail. We found that culturally different families interacted around familiar expository texts, like toy advertisements, the way in which middle class families do around traditional expository trade books because the design features of the texts were similar, i.e. both had labeled pictures not unified linguistically by a common theme. Expository texts, then, are a specific literacy context with specific rules. This genre in a familiar format (i.e. toy advertisements from the local paper) elicits the same interaction styles for non-mainstream families that characterize the book reading behavior of mainstream families.

There are at least two other important implications of the genre and format effects on mother–child interaction. First, teachers and researchers should be cognizant of genre effects. Both children and adults do very different things with different genres. Second, from an educational perspective, if our goal is to facilitate adult–child interaction around books, expositories in familiar formats are more readily used in this way. If we believe, following the zone of proximal development, that children's learning is the result of joint engagement with adults in activities, then expository texts are particularly useful to the extent that they maximize joint participation.

Children's reading or participation?

Also following Cazden (1970) and the Laboratory of Comparative Human Cognition (1983), we advocate a rather different way of assessing children in the joint reading contexts. Rather than looking only at children's ability to decode or comprehend text, a more sensitive index of children's literacy, we would argue, is to examine the extent to which they *participate* in the joint reading event and the level of adult support necessary for that participation. Children's level of task participation is the assessment form consistent with the zone of proximal development (Brown *et al.*, 1983; Pellegrini *et al.*, 1985a, 1985b, 1990; Vygotsky, 1978). In learning higher order cognitive processes, according to Vygotsky's theory, children interact around a specific task with adults. By participating in these joint activities children learn by becoming involved in and contributing to the tasks. Previous research has documented the validity of task participation as a measure of task competence (Brown *et al.*, 1983; Pellegrini *et al.*, 1985a, 1985b). Relevant to joint reading, measures of children's participation include making text relevant initiations (e.g. 'What's this?'), relating elements of the text being read to psychologically distant stimuli (e.g. 'Max the wild child is a king too') and text relevant responses to mother (e.g. Mother asks: 'What's here?' and child responds: 'A pelican').

In conjunction with children's level of task participation it is also imperative to consider the amount of support adults provide so that children can participate. Obviously, the two are interrelated. Children who exhibit more task involvement with minimal adult support are more competent in that task than children who exhibit similar levels of participation with more adult support. Our work and the work of Ann Brown (e.g. Brown *et al.*, 1983) has shown that these child and adult criteria are more sensitive indices of learning than more traditional measures, such as number of comprehension answers correct.

Again, this approach is intuitively sensible. Consider the teacher who has her class independently reading a text and answering questions at the end of the chapter. In this class one child, Max, must be reminded by the teacher to open his book to the correct page, to use the appropriate question booklet, and to only answer the questions at the end of the chapter. Max answers seventeen of the twenty questions correctly. Another child in the class, Anna, listens to the teacher's directions to the class, reads the appropriate pages, answers the questions, and also scores seventeen out of twenty. Are these children equally competent in the task?

A developmental perspective, however, should be applied to this context-specific approach. This involves mapping changes within individuals across time, with a basic assumption being that the skills and concepts *within* each developmental period are evaluated according to period specific criteria, not criteria in another period.

The specifics of literacy instruction

In designing the ideal instructional world, we should begin by considering the design features of the school activity in relation to relevant activities of our students. By activity here, we mean, following Leontiev (1978) and the Laboratory of Comparative Human Cognition (1983), the motives, goals and conclusions of a setting.

We must look at the specific processes that mothers and their children use as they interact around texts. Around expository texts, like toy ads, mothers and children both initiate interaction and ask questions. Children are encouraged to relate aspects of the text to the outside world, as well as to answer questions about the text. The more general interaction rule, however, seems to be that mothers try to maximize children's participation in the task. They do this by gauging their levels of interaction to the child's level; for example, mothers often start off a session by asking a cognitively demanding question, such as, 'Can this really happen?' and, next, pose a less demanding question, such as, 'What's this?' if children do not respond appropriately. Through such interactions, children and mothers define the essence of a literacy event. It may involve identifying toys advertised in the newspaper and who else in their neighborhood might have one. In all cases, joint participation seems to characterize the process.

The last level of analysis involves the ways in which children are taught to take meaning from the text. Following the context-specific orientation, we believe that ways of taking meaning from text are different for different groups interacting around different forms of text (Bruner, 1986; Heath, 1982, 1983). The model which best captures the ways in which cultural meaning is constructed and transmitted is described by Vygotsky's (1978) notion of the zone of proximal development. The values of the culture, or in this case the rules of literacy events, are learned by joint participation. Mothers that we observed had a specific way of interacting around text, e.g. asking children to relate text-based information to the outside world. For the child just learning the rules, mothers model appropriate behavior and encourage participation by relatively non-demanding strategies, such as repetition. A more competent child may be asked about a picture, for example, 'Is this like Lonnie's?' Children who are yet more competent often initiate interaction, e.g. 'Those at school too.' In short, children are cultural apprentices wherein they and mother construct the rules governing literacy events.

Different activities should be characterized by different rules. So, the teacher of the non-mainstream child must identify children's knowledge of the rules of different literacy events and the extent to which these rules differ from those of school-based events. This knowledge is necessary to design our school curriculum.

Now that we know the design features of the literacy events at home we can design school-based literacy events. Our goal is to maximize the transfer from the home to the school events. An overriding concern with this approach, as in most cases where transfer is the goal, is to repeatedly remind students of the similarities between school and home literacy events where they exist; e.g. in both cases children are asked to volunteer information and to relate aspects of text to the external world. A second important concern involves the maximizing of children's participation in the school literacy events, as noted above. Children learn the register of school literacy events by participating in events using it. Maximum participation of both children and teachers occurs around expository texts. Consequently, we recommend that, initially, children be exposed to familiar expository texts. The expository texts that are actually used in students' homes should be the basis for joint reading. When teachers interact with children around these texts, it also would be useful to keep in mind the interaction rules of children's home reading events. When we observed children and mothers interacting around familiar format texts they used interactions strategies typically observed in middle class families; e.g. mothers gauge their teaching styles to children's level of competence and maximize children's task participation.

Next, children and teachers could make expository texts that relate to the classroom; for example, photographs of the classroom and the school could be taken, labeled and bound into books which are then used in joint reading sessions. Trade books that demand similar interaction styles can be used next. Of course, the content of the book must be familiar. Trade books that label components of classrooms would serve this function in light of the preceding text recommended.

Y'All Know What?

In this section we examine another literacy event which is important in children learning the rules of school-based literacy. This event, labeled 'Y'All Know What?', is similar to 'sharing time' in classrooms where children talk about personal experiences and relate them to their whole classroom. We have shown in this book the importance of school 'community' and close relationships (in the form of friendships) in maximizing success in school-based literacy.

Sara Michaels (1981) was one of the first scholars to illustrate the importance of sharing time in learning the rules of school-based discourse, particularly those related to narratives. Narratives, both personal and public, self-constructed and constructed by others, played a central role in one classroom we observed, and the details of which are described in greater detail in Chapter 5. It was through narrative that children intermingled their home lives and their school lives. Narrative also allowed them to go beyond their lives to share those of their classmates, their teachers and the characters about whom they read. Narrative was the primary means by which this community constructed itself.

'Y'All Know What?' was probably effective because it was a bridge from a rather familiar and indigenous speech event to the more literate discourse of school. Betty, the teacher in this classroom, began her day with 'Y'All Know What?' time, an oral sharing session that evolved across the year. During this time the child who had the floor began by saying, 'Y'All know what?' After the class naturally responded with 'What?' the speaker went on to tell his or her story. Betty accepted all contributions with a positive response, setting the stage for the borrowing of ideas that was to become so crucial to the life in this classroom. After a relatively short period speakers perched on a stool, holding the microphone, talking to a rapt audience and it was evident that the children have begun to display a personal style, relate oral language to their writing, and borrow ideas, language and structures from each other. These things originated with the children's oral storytelling, but Betty made them explicit, helping the children to see what they, as a group, already knew how to do.

Often this elaboration led to restructuring the instructional plans. One child's (Rick) story, and Betty's remark about his 'tall tale', immediately began an exploration of the tall tale subgenre through book and video, and led a number of children into their own tall tales. Within a month, tall tales became such a popular subgenre in this community that children would often preface their oral storytelling or introduce their writing during sharing time with 'I'm gonna tell a tall tale' or, 'I wrote a tall tale.' This peaked in October, but remained an available option for the rest of the year.

As the children changed and the classroom community developed, 'Y'All Know What?' changed over time from a forum for sharing home lives with school companions and for rehearsing potential ideas for writing to a time to retell familiar stories, demonstrating to all the skill of the storyteller and engaging the audience in a happy recreation of a familiar tale.

Building on the confidence generated during the early days of 'Y'All Know What?', after winter break Betty gradually moved the children toward more formal uses of narrative language, helping them to make the polished prose of children's trade books their own in a way that in no way diminished the value of their natural language. Just as they adopted a particular register for their sharing of stories from home when they uttered their introductory 'Y'All Know What?', Betty's students adopted the register of the accomplished storyteller when they began to retell familiar tales. They grew in confidence and expertise during February and March, and by April were assured, polished storytellers.

'Y'All Know What?', and the stories that it produced, was the primary, but not only, way in which children brought their lives from home and offered them as resources for the classroom community. By demonstrating how she could talk about her own life, by inviting children to talk about theirs, and by affirming what they said and offering it to others, Betty stressed the importance of the dailiness of children's lives. Bringing their lives into the classroom through personal narrative, Betty and her students did what we all do: they made sense of their lives through story. This planned-for sense-making had a number of results.

First, their personal narratives connected their home lives to their school life, blurring the distinction between home and school that the schoolhouse door too often makes. This affirmed the value and importance that individual children had in this classroom, making them feel cherished and integral to the life there.

Second, the children used their oral narratives as a way of getting to know each other and building their community. They quickly discovered similarities in their lives while they also discovered who was expert in what. Knowing that one child (Brooke) liked horses, knew a lot about them, and could draw them well made Brooke the horse expert for the entire school year. The knowledge of and respect for each other that 'Y'All Know What?' engendered was reflected in the collaborative nature of literacy events in the classroom.

Third, children's personal narratives also offered material for the reading and writing they did in the classroom. They used their own oral stories as sources for ideas to write about; they also used the oral stories of their classmates as sources for ideas. Ami, for example, told the class about how sad her neighbor was when her dog got hit by a car. By sharing this story with others Ami explored it for herself, was assured that she now knew something about how sadness looked that she could remember and think about when she wanted to write about being sad, and gave the others in the class ideas for their own writing as they in turn remembered their own sad times. Sometimes children used their oral narratives to rehearse directly what they were going to write about, announcing their intentions to 'write about' what they were telling even as they were engaged in the telling.

Although 'Y'All Know What?' was a central force in the building of community and the development of literacy in this classroom, it wasn't the only opportunity that the children had to talk together and learn from each other. The children had freedom of choice and movement during reading time in the morning, choosing any of the hundreds of books that filled the room. On any given day you would see children reading in many places in the room – a big cardboard box used as a model covered wagon for their study of 'the old days', a corner, the stage area, their tables, under Betty's desk, in the hall – and in many social configurations. Brooke and Jennay often read together, Pakaysahn, Jason and Jennay usually read independently but in close proximity to each other. Andrew and Marienesha often found each other and read together but would also read independently. Jennay's favorite spot for most of the fall and winter was in the box surrounded by stuffed animals which she propped up ready to listen to the story that she read aloud to them. The frequent whole class read aloud offered a different social configuration, bringing everyone together to share story and commentary, building shared knowledge around a storybook.

Writing time, too, offered opportunities for and rested on collaboration as children worked at small tables with three to five companions.

> Sheri shows me [LG] an empty page. I ask, 'What are you going to do with these pages?' She replies, 'I'm gonna write "balloons"', and goes on to draw a balloon. When she asks, 'How do you spell Ms. Shockley?', Kimberly jumps up and gets a book, returning with it open to the inside page, saying, 'Here's how to spell Shockley. Just go get a book that her name is on and copy it. Her name is on all of the books in the classroom.'
>
> (Fieldnotes, September 1)

> Children are scattered throughout the room with papers, pencils, books, and markers. Everyone is engaged in writing. There is a hum of talk as children ask, of those with whom they are sitting, how to spell words. Various children offer spellings and discuss which one is correct, the writer puts down what she considers the best, and then goes on. Children are murmuring to themselves,

talking with Betty, the aide, and me. Suddenly Ami bursts into song. Other children pick up her song and continue their writing, singing.

(Fieldnotes, October 7)

Ami's song, joined by her classmates, demonstrates the degree of comfort that the children felt as they worked in their classroom.

Conclusion

In this chapter we present ideas for improving literacy instruction, particularly for children who typically fail in this area. An important assumption in this work, as in our own research, is recognition of the fact that school-based literacy and literate language are both language variants which are not better or worse than other variants but having access to them also provides access to power, resources and increased probability of success in school. We teach school-based literacy and language as registers to be used in schools to provide access to those resources.

From these basic assumptions about school-based literacy we discuss two examples, based on the research presented in the book. First, we discuss the ways in which joint book reading can be used as a way in which children learn the vocabulary and behaviors associated with school-based literacy. This can best be accomplished by first exposing children to types of texts with which they are most familiar. Later, less familiar texts can be presented, taking special care to point out similarities and differences between the texts.

We also presented ways in which peers can be helpful in teaching literacy. Unlike many extant models of peer teaching we suggest that the children's close relationships with peers may maximize learning. Rather than separating friends during instructional periods, as some teachers may be tempted to do, we suggest that children should be placed with their friends and encouraged, not discouraged, to interact.

References

Adams, M. J. (1990) *Beginning to Read*. Cambridge, MA: MIT Press.

Anderson, A., Teale, W. and Estrada, E. (1980) 'Low-income children's preschool literary experiences: some naturalistic observations'. *Quarterly Newsletter of the Laboratory of Comparative Human Cognition* **2**, 59–65.

Anderson, R., Wilson, P. and Fielding, L. (1988) 'Growth in reading and how children spend their time outside of school'. *Reading Research Quarterly* **23**, 285–303.

Applebee, A. (1978) *The Child's Concept of Story*. Chicago: University of Chicago Press.

Arsenio, W. F. and Killen, M. (1996) 'Conflict-related emotions during peer disputes'. *Early Education and Development* **7**, 43–57.

Au, K. and Kawakami, A. (1984) 'Vygotskian perspectives on discussion processes in small group reading lessons', in P. Peterson, L. C. Wilkinson and M. Hallinan (eds) *The Social Context of Instruction* (pp. 209–228). New York: Academic Press.

Azimitia, M. and Montgomery, R. (1993) 'Friendship, transactive dialogues, and the development of scientific reasoning'. *Social Development* **2**, 202–221.

Bakeman, R. and Brownlee, J. (1980) 'The strategic use of parallel play: a sequential analysis'. *Child Development* **51**, 873–878.

Bakeman, R. and Gottman, J. M. (1986) *Observing Interaction: An Introduction to Sequential Analysis*. New York: Cambridge University Press.

Bandura, A. (1986) *Social Foundations of Thought and Action*. Englewood Cliffs, NJ: Prentice-Hall.

Bateson, P. P. G. (1976) 'Rules and reciprocity in behavioural development', in P. P. G. Bateson and R. A. Hinde (eds) *Growing Points in Ecology* (pp. 401–421). Cambridge: Cambridge University Press.

Bateson, P. P. G. (1981) 'Discontinuities in development and changes in the organization of play in cats', in K. Immelmann, G. Barlow, L. Petronovich and M. Main (eds) *Behavioural Development* (pp. 281–295). Cambridge: Cambridge University Press.

Baumrind, D. (1989) 'Rearing competent children', in W. Damon (ed.) *Child Development Today and Tomorrow* (pp. 349–378). San Francisco, CA: Jossey-Bass.

Bekoff, M. and Byers, J. A. (1981) 'A critical re-analysis of the ontogeny and phylogeny of mammalian social and locomotor play', in K. Immelmann, G. Barlow, L. Petronovich and M. Main (eds) *Behavioural Development* (pp. 296–337). Cambridge: Cambridge University Press.

Bell, R. Q. (1979) 'Parent, child, and reciprocal influences'. *American Psychologist* **10**, 821–826.

Bernstein, B. (1960) 'Language and social class'. *British Journal of Sociology* **2**, 217–276.

Bernstein, B. (1971) *Class, Codes, and Control*, vol. 1. London: Routledge and Kegan Paul.

Bernstein, B. (1972) 'Social class, language, and socialization', in P. Giglioli (ed.) *Language and Social Context* (pp. 157–178). Harmondsworth: Penguin.

Bernstein, B. (1982) 'Codes, modalities and the process of cultural reproduction: a model', in M. Apple (ed.) *Cultural and Economic Reproduction in Education*. Boston, MA: Routledge and Kegan Paul.

Bjorklund, D. and Green, B. (1992) 'The adaptive nature of cognitive immaturity'. *American Psychologist* **47**, 46–54.

Bloch, M. (1989) 'Young boys' and girls' play in the home and in the community: a cultural ecological framework', in M. Bloch and A. D. Pellegrini (eds) *The Ecological Context of Children's Play* (pp. 120–154). Norwood, NJ: Ablex.

Block, J. (1983) 'Differential premises arising from differential socialization of the sexes: some conjectures'. *Child Development* **54**, 1354–1365.

Boulton, M. J. and Smith, P. K. (1992) 'The social nature of play-fighting and play-chasing: mechanisms and strategies underlying cooperation and compromise', in J. H. Barlow, L. Cosmides and J. Tooby (eds) *The Adapted Mind* (pp. 429–444). New York: Oxford University Press.

Bradley, L. and Bryant, P. (1983) 'Categorizing sounds and learning to read: a causal connection'. *Nature* **301**, 419–421.

Britton, J. (1970) *Language and Learning*. Harmondsworth: Penguin.

Brody, G. H., Stoneman, Z. and McCoy, K. (1994) 'Forecasting sibling relationships in early adolescence from childhood temperaments and family processes in middle childhood'. *Child Development* **65**, 771–784.

Bronfennbrenner, U. (1979) *The Ecology of Human Development*. Cambridge, MA: Harvard University Press.

Brown, A. L., Bransford, J. D., Ferrara, R. A. and Campione, J. C. (1983) 'Learning, remembering, and understanding', in J. H. Flavell and E. M. Markman (eds) *Handbook of Child Psychology*, vol. 3: *Cognitive Development* (pp. 77–166). New York: Wiley.

Brown, M. (1989) *Arthur's Birthday*. New York: Houghton-Mifflin.

Bruner, J. S. (1986) *Actual Minds, Possible Worlds*. Cambridge, MA: Harvard University Press.

Burns, S. and Brainerd, C. (1979) 'Effects of constructive and dramatic play on perspective taking in very young children'. *Developmental Psychology* **15**, 512–521.

Bus, A. G. and vanIJzendoorn, M. H. (1988) 'Mother–child interaction, attachment, and emergent literacy: a cross-sectional study'. *Child Development* **59**, 1262–1273.

Bus, A. G. and vanIJzendoorn, M. H. (1995) 'Mothers reading to their 3-year-olds: the role of mother–child attachment security in becoming literate'. *Reading Research Quarterly* **30**, 998–1015.

Bus, A. G., vanIJzendoorn, M. H. and Pellegrini, A. D. (1995) 'Joint book reading makes for success in learning to read: a meta-analysis on intergenerational transmission of literacy'. *Review of Educational Research* **65**, 1–21.

Caldwell, B. and Bradley, R. (1984) 'The HOME observation for measurement of the environment', unpublished manuscript, Little Rock, AK.

Calkins, L.M. (1991) *Living between the Lines*. Portsmouth, NH: Heinemann.

Campos, J. J., Barrett, K. C., Lamb, M., Goldsmith, H. and Stenberg, C. (1983) 'Socioemotional development', in M. M. Haith and J. J. Campos (eds) *Handbook of Child Psychology*, vol. 2 (pp. 783–916). New York: Wiley.

Caro, T. (1982) 'The energy cost of play: definition and estimation'. *Animal Behaviour* **30**, 294–295.

Caro, T. (1988) 'Adaptive significance of play: are we getting closer?' *Trends in Ecology and Evolution* **3**, 50–54.

Caro, T. (1995) 'Short-term costs and correlates of play in cheetahs'. *Animal Behaviour* **49**, 333–345.

Cazden, C. B. (1965) 'Environmental assistance to the child's acquisition of grammar', unpublished doctoral dissertation, Harvard University, Cambridge, MA.

Cazden, C. B. (1970) 'The situation: a neglected source of social class differences in language use'. *Journal of Social Issues* **26**, 35–59.

Chandler, M. (1973) 'Egocentrism and antisocial behavior'. *Developmental Psychology* **9**, 326–332.

Clark, G. (1992) *How Many Days to My Birthday?* New York: Houghton-Mifflin.

Clark, M. (1976) *Young Fluent Readers*. London: Heinemann.

Clay, M. (1977) *Reading: The Patterning of Complex Behaviour*. London: Heinemann.

Clay, M. (1985) *Concepts about Print*. Auckland, NZ: Heinemann.

Cochran, M. and Riley, D. (1988) 'Mother reports of children's personal networks', in S. Salzinger, J. Antrobus and M. Hammer (eds) *Social Networks of Children* (pp. 131–147). Hillsdale, NJ: Erlbaum.

Cochran-Smith, M. (1984) *The Making of a Reader*. Norwood, NJ: Ablex.

Cook-Gumperz, J. (1973) *Social Control and Socialization*. London: Routledge and Kegan Paul.

Cook-Gumperz, J. (1982) 'Situated instructions', in S. Ervin-Tripp and C. Mitchell-Kernan (eds) *Child Discourse* (pp. 103–124). New York: Academic Press.

Cornell, E., Senechal, M. and Broda, L. (1988) 'Recall of picture books by 3-year-old children'. *Journal and Educational Psychology* **80**, 537–542.

Crambit, N. and Siegel, G. (1977) 'The verbal environment of a language impaired'. *Child Journal of Speech and Hearing Disorders* **42**, 474–482.

Cullinan, B. E. and Galda, L. (1998) *Literature and the Child*, 3rd edn. Fort Worth, TX: Harcourt Brace.

Daiute, C., Hartup, W., Sholl, W. and Zajac, R. (1993) 'Peer collaboration and written language'. Paper presented at the biennial meetings of the Society for Research in Child Development, New Orleans, March.

Darwin, C. (1977) 'Biographical sketch of an infant'. *Mind* **2**, 285–294.

DeLoach, J. S. and Mendoza, O. A. P. (1987) 'Joint picture book interactions of mothers and 1-year-old children'. *British Journal of Developmental Psychology* **5**, 111–123.

Delpit, L. (1990) 'Language diversity and language learning', in S. Hynds and D. L. Rubin (eds) *Perspective on Talk and Learning*. Urbana, IL: National Council of Teachers of English.

DeStefano, J. S. (1984) 'Learning to communicate in the classroom', in A. D. Pellegrini and T. D. Yawkey (eds) *The Development of Oral and Written Language in Social Contexts* (pp. 155–165). Norwood, NJ: Ablex.

DeTemple, J. M. and Beals, D. E. (1991) 'Family talk'. Paper presented at the annual meeting of the American Educational Research Association, Chicago.

Dickinson, D. and Moreton, J. (1991) 'Predicting specific kindergarten literacy skills from three-year-olds' preschool experiences'. Paper presented at the Society for Research in Child Development, Seattle, April.

Dickinson, D. K. and Smith, M. (1994) 'Long term effects of preschool teachers' book reading on low income children's vocabulary, story comprehension, and print skills'. *Reading Research Quarterly* **29**, 104–123.

Dickinson, D. K., DeTemple, J. M., Hirschler, J. A. and Smith, M. (1992) 'Book reading with preschoolers: construction of text at home and at school'. *Early Childhood Research Quarterly* **7**, 323–346.

Dunn, J. (1988) *The Beginning of Social Understanding*. Cambridge, MA: Harvard University Press.

Dunn, J. and Slomkowski, C. (1992) 'Conflict and the development of social understanding', in C. U. Shantz and W. W. Hartup (eds) *Conflict in Child and Adolescent Development* (pp. 70–92). Cambridge: Cambridge University Press.

Dunn, L. and Dunn, L. (1981) *Peabody Picture Vocabulary Test*. Circle Pines, MN: American Guidance Services.

Durkin, D. (1966) *Children Who Read Early*. New York: Teachers College Press.

Fagen, R. (1981) *Animal Play Behavior*. New York: Oxford University Press.

Falk, R. F. and Miller, N. B. (1991) *A Primer for Soft Modeling*. Toledo, OH: University of Toledo Press.

Faulkner, W. (1961) *The Town*. New York: Random House.

Fein, G. (1979) 'Play and the acquisition of symbols', in L. Katz (ed.) *Current Topics in Early Childhood Education* (pp. 195–225). Norwood, NJ: Ablex.

Fein, G. (1981) 'Pretend play: an integrative review'. *Child Development* **52**, 1095–1118.

Freeman, D. (1966) *A Rainbow of My Own*. New York: Viking.

Fribas, J. (1966) 'On defining the theme in functional sentence analysis'. *Travaux Linguistudies de Prague* **1**, 267–280.

Galda, L. (1984) 'Play, story telling, and story comprehension: narrative competence', in A. D. Pellegrini and T. D. Yawkey (eds) *The Development of Oral and Written Language in Social Context* (pp. 105–115). Norwood, NJ: Ablex.

Galda, L., Cullinan, B. and Strickland, D. (1997) *Language, Literacy, and the Child*, 2nd edn. Fort Worth, TX: Harcourt, Brace, Jovanovich.

Galda, L., Bisplinghoff, B. S. and Pellegrini, A. D. (1996) *Literacy in Transition*, National Reading Research Center Reading Research Report, **62**.

Garvey, C. (1984) *Children's Talk*. Cambridge, MA: Harvard University Press.

Garvey, C. (1990) *Play*. Cambridge, MA: Harvard University Press.

Garvey, C. and Kramer, T. L. (1989) 'The language of social pretend'. *Merrill-Palmer Quarterly* **9**, 364–382.

Garvey, C. and Shantz, C. U. (1992) 'Conflict talk: approaches adversative discourse', in C. U. Shantz and W. Hartup (eds) *Conflict in Childhood and Adolescence* (pp. 93–121). New York: Cambridge University Press.

Gee, J. P. (1989) *Journal of Education* **171** (1), whole number.

Gomendio, M. (1988) 'The development of different types of play in gazelles: implications for the nature and functions of play'. *Animal Behaviour* **36**, 825–836.

Groos, K. (1898) *The Play of Animals*. New York: Appleton.

Groos, K. (1901) *The Play of Man*. New York: Appleton.

Gumperz, J. (1986) 'Interactional sociolinguistics in the study of schooling', in J Cook-Gumperz (ed.) *The Social Construction of Literacy* (pp. 45–68). London: Cambridge University Press.

Haight, W. L. and Miller, P. J. (1993) *Pretending at Home*. Albany, NY: State University of New York Press.

Halliday, M. A. K. (1967) 'Notes on transitivity and theme in English, Part 2'. *Journal of Linguistics* **3**, 177–274.

Halliday, M. A. K. (1969–70) 'Relevant models of language'. *Educational Review* **22**, 26–37.

Halliday, M. A. K. and Hasan, R. (1976) *Cohesion in English*. London: Longman.

Harman, I. (1970) 'Illiteracy: an overview'. *Harvard Educational Review* **40**, 226–243.

Hartup, W. W. (1983) 'Peer relations', in E. M. Hetherington (ed.) *Handbook in Child Psychology*, vol. 4 (pp. 103–196). New York: Wiley.

Hartup, W. W. (1992) 'Conflict and friendship relations', in C. U. Shantz and W. W. Hartup (eds) *Conflict in Child and Adolescent Development* (pp. 186–215). Cambridge: Cambridge University Press.

Hartup, W. W. (1996) 'The company they keep: friendships and their developmental significance'. *Child Development* **67**, 1–13.

Hartup, W., French, D., Laursen, B., Johnston, K. and Ogawa, J. (1993) 'Conflict and friendship relations in middle childhood: behavior in a closed-field situation'. *Child Development* **64**, 445–454.

Heath, S. B. (1982) 'What no bedtime story means: narrative skill at home and school'. *Language in Society* **1**, 49–76.

Heath, S. B. (1983) *Ways with Words*. Cambridge: Cambridge University Press.

Heath, S. B. (1989) 'Oral and literate traditions among black Americans living in poverty'. *American Psychologist* **44**, 367–373.

Hess, R.D. and Shipman, V. C. (1965) 'Early experience and the socialization of cognitive modes in children'. *Child Development* **36**, 369–386.

Hinde, R. A. (1978) 'On describing relationships'. *Journal of Child Psychology and Psychiatry* **17**, 1–19.

Hinde, R. A. (1980) *Ethology*. London: Fontana.

Hinde, R. A., Stevenson-Hinde, J. and Tamplin, A. (1985) 'Characteristics of 3- and 4-year-olds assessed at home and their interactions in preschool'. *Developmental Psychology* **21**, 130–140.

Hollander, M. and Wolfe, D. A. (1973) *Nonparametric Statistical Methods*. New York: Wiley.

Howes, C. (1993) *The Collaborative Construction of Pretense*. Albany, NY: State University of New York Press.

Hymes, D. (1967) 'Models of the interaction of language and social setting'. *Journal of Social Issues* **23**, 8–28.

Jones, I. and Pellegrini, A. D. (1996) 'The effects of social relationships, writing media, and microgenetic development on first grade students' narratives'. *American Educational Research Journal* **33**, 691–718.

Kagan, J. (1971) *Change and Continuity in Infancy*. New York: Wiley.

Kagan, J. (1983) 'Classification of the child', in W. Kessen (ed.) *Handbook of Child Psychology*, vol. 1 (pp. 527–560). New York: Wiley.

Kramer, T. L., Bukowski, W. M. and Garvey, C. (1989) 'The influence of dyadic context on the conversational and linguistic behavior of its members'. *Merrill-Palmer Quarterly* **35**, 327–341.

Laboratory of Comparative Human Cognition (1983) 'Culture and cognitive development', in W. Kessen (ed.) *Handbook of Child Psychology*, vol. 1 (pp. 295–352). New York: Wiley.

Leonard, L. (1982) 'The nature of specific language impairment with children', in S. Rosenberg (ed.) *Handbook of Applied Psycholinguistics* (pp. 295–327). Hillsdale, NJ: Erlbaum.

Leontiev, A. (1978) *Activity, Consciousness, and Personality*. Englewood Cliffs, NJ: Prentice-Hall.

Lerner, R. (1984) *On the Nature of Human Plasticity*. New York: Cambridge University Press.

Lewin, K. (1946) 'Behavior and development as a function of the total situation', in L. Carmichael (ed.) *Manual of Child Psychology*, 1st edn (pp. 791–844). New York: Wiley.

Maccoby, E. (1990) 'Gender and relationships: a developmental account'. *American Psychologist* **45**, 513–520.

McLoyd, V. (1980) 'Verbal expressed modes of transformations in the fantasy and play of Black preschool children'. *Child Development* 51, 1133–1139.

Martin, P. and Bateson, P. (1993) *Measuring Behaviour*. London: Cambridge University Press.

Martin, P. and Caro, T. (1985) 'On the function of play and its role in behavioral development', in J. Rosenblatt, C. Beer, M. Busnel, and P. Slater (eds) *Advances in the Study of Behavior*, vol. 15 (pp. 59–103). New York: Academic Press.

Martin, R. P. (1988) *The Temperament Assesment Battery for Children: Teacher's Form*. Brandon, VT: Clinical Psychology Press.

Martin, R. P., Drew, K. D., Gaddis, L. A. and Moseley, M. (1988) 'Prediction of elementary school achievement from preschool temperament: three studies'. *School Psychology Review* **17**, 125–137.

Michaels, S. (1981) 'Sharing time: children's styles and access to literacy'. *Language in Society* **10**, 423–442.

Murray, F. (1972) 'Acquisition of conservation through social interaction'. *Developmental Psychology* **6**, 1–6.

Ninio, A. (1980a) 'Picture book reading in mother–infant dyads belong to two subgroups in Israel'. *Child Development* **51**, 587–590.

Ninio, A. (1980b) 'Ostensive definition in vocabulary teaching'. *Journal of Child Language* **7**, 565–573.

Ninio, A. (1983) 'Joint book reading as a multiple vocabulary acquisition device'. *Developmental Psychology* **19**, 445–451.

Ninio, A. and Bruner, J. S. (1978) 'The achievement and antecedents of labeling'. *Journal of Child Language* **3**, 1–15.

Ogbu, J. (1981) 'Origins of human competence: a cultural ecological perspective'. *Child Development* **52**, 413–429.

Olson, D. R. (1977) 'From utterance to text: the literate bias of language in speech and writing'. *Harvard Educational Review* **47**, 257–281.

Parten, M. (1932) 'Social participation among preschool children'. *Journal of Abnormal and Social Psychology* **27**, 243–269.

Pellegrini, A. D. (1980) 'The relationship between kindergarteners' play and achievement in pre-reading, language, and writing'. *Psychology in the Schools* **17**, 530–535.

Pellegrini, A. D. (1981) 'The development of preschoolers' private speech'. *Journal of Pragmatics* **5**, 278–292.

Pellegrini, A. D. (1982) 'The generation of cohesive text by preschoolers in two play contexts'. *Discourse Processes* **5**, 101–108.

Pellegrini, A. D. (1983) 'Sociolinguistic contexts of the preschool'. *Journal of Applied Developmental Psychology* **4**, 389–397.

Pellegrini, A. D. (1984a) 'The social cognitive ecology of preschool classrooms'. *International Journal of Behavioural Development* **7**, 321–332.

Pellegrini, A. D. (1984b) 'Identifying causal elements in the thematic fantasy play paradigm'. *American Educational Research Journal* **21**, 691–703.

Pellegrini, A. D. (1985) 'Relations between preschool children's symbolic play and literate behavior', in L. Galda and A. D. Pellegrini (eds) *Play, Language, and Stories* (pp. 79–98). Norwood, NJ: Ablex.

Pellegrini, A. D. (1986) 'Play center and the production of imaginative language'. *Discourse Processes* **9**, 1–9.

Pellegrini, A. D. (1988) 'Elementary school children's rough-and-tumble play and social competence'. *Developmental Psychology* **24**, 802–806.

Pellegrini, A. D. (1996) *Observing Children in the Natural Worlds: A Methological Primer*. Mahwah, NJ: Erlbaum.

Pellegrini, A. D. and Davis, P. (1993) 'Relations between children's playground and classroom behaviour'. *British Journal of Educational Psychology* **63**, 86–95.

Pellegrini, A. D. and Galda, L. (1988) 'The effects of age and context on children's use of narrative language'. *Research in the Teaching of English* **22**, 183–195.

Pellegrini, A. D. and Galda, L. (1991) 'Longitudinal relations among preschoolers' symbolic play, metalinguistic verbs, and emergent literacy', in J. Christie (ed.) *Play and Early Literacy Development* (pp. 47–68). Albany, NY: State University of New York Press.

Pellegrini, A. D. and Galda, L. (1993) 'Ten years after: a re-examination of symbolic play and literacy research'. *Reading Research Quarterly* **28**, 163–175.

Pellegrini, A. D. and Horvat, M. (1995) 'A developmental contextualist critique of Attention Deficit Hyperactivity Disorder (ADHD)'. *Educational Researcher* **24**, 13–20.

Pellegrini, A. D. and Perlmutter, J. C. (1987) 'A re-examination of the Smilansky–Parten matrix of play behaviors'. *Journal of Research in Childhood Education* **2**, 89–96.

Pellegrini, A. D. and Perlmutter, J. C. (1989) 'Classroom contextual effects on children's play'. *Developmental Psychology* **25**, 289–296.

Pellegrini, A. D. and Stanic, G. M. A. (1993) 'Locating children's mathematical competence: application of the developmental niche'. *Journal of Applied Developmental Psychology* **14**, 501–520.

Pellegrini, A. D., Galda, L. and Rubin, D. (1984a) 'Context in text: the development of oral and written language in two genres'. *Child Development* **55**, 1549–1555.

Pellegrini, A. D., Galda, L. and Rubin, D. (1984b) 'Persuasion as a social cognitive activity'. *Language and Communication* **4**, 285–293.

Pellegrini, A. D., Brody, G. H. and Sigel, I. E. (1985a) 'Parents' bookreading habits with their children'. *Journal of Educational Psychology* **77**, 332–340.

Pellegrini, A. D., Brody, G. H. and Sigel, I. E. (1985b) 'Parents' teaching strategies with their children'. *Journal of Psycholinguistic Research* **14**, 509–521.

Pellegrini, A. D., Perlmutter, J. C., Galda, L. and Brody, G. H. (1990) 'Joint bookreading between Black Head Start children and their mothers'. *Child Development* **61**, 443–453.

Pellegrini, A. D., Galda, L., Stahl, S. and Shockley, B. (1995a) 'The nexus of social and literacy experiences at home and school: implications for primary school oral language and literacy'. *British Journal of Educational Psychology* **65**, 273–285.

Pellegrini, A. D., Galda, L., Jones, I. and Perlmutter, J. C. (1995b) 'Joint reading between mothers and their Head Start children: vocabulary learning in two text formats'. *Discourse Processes* **19**, 441–463.

Pellegrini, A. D., Huberty, P. D. and Jones, I. (1995c) 'The effects of recess timing on children's playground and classroom behaviors'. *American Educational Research Journal* **32**, 845–864.

Pellegrini, A. D., Galda, L., Bartini, M. and Charak, D. (1998) 'Oral language and literacy learning in context: the role of social relationships'. *Merrill-Palmer Quarterly* **44**, 38–45.

Piaget, J. (1962) *Play, Dreams, and Imitation*. New York: Norton.

Piaget, J. (1983) 'Piaget's theory', in W. Kessen (ed.) *Handbook of Child Psychology*, vol. 1 (pp. 103–128). New York: Wiley.

Rubin, K. H. (1980) 'Fantasy play: its role in the development of social skills and social cognition', in K. H. Rubin (ed.) *Children's Play* (pp. 69–84). San Francisco, CA: Jossey-Bass.

Rubin, K. H. and Clarke, L. (1982) 'Preschool teachers' ratings of behavior problems'. Paper presented at the annual meeting of the American Educational Research Association, New York.

Rubin, K. H., Fein, G. and Vandenberg, B. (1983) 'Play', in E. M. Hetherington (ed.) *Handbook of Child Psychology*, vol. 4: *Socialization, Personality, and Social Development* (pp. 693–774). New York: Wiley.

Rubin, K. H., Maioni, T. and Hornung, H. (1976) 'Free play in middle and lower class preschoolers: Parten and Piaget revisited'. *Child Development* **47**, 414–419.

Rubin, K. H., Watson, R. and Jambor, T. (1978) 'Free play behaviors in preschool and kindergarten children'. *Child Development* **49**, 534–546.

Rushton, J., Brainerd, C. and Pressley, M. (1983) 'Behavioral development and construct validity: the principle of aggregation'. *Psychological Bulletin* **94**, 18–38.

Rylant, C. (1987) *Birthday Presents*. New York: Orchard.

Sackett, G. P., Sameroff, A. J., Cairns, R. B. and Suomi, S. J. (1981) 'Continuity in behavioral development: theoretical and empirical issues', in K. Immelmann, G. Barlow, L. Petrinovich, and M. Main (eds) *Behavioral Development* (pp. 23–57). London: Cambridge University Press.

Scarborough, H. S. and Dobrich, W. (1994) 'On the efficacy of reading to preschoolers'. *Developmental Review* **14**, 245–302.

Schieffelin, B. and Cochran-Smith, M. (1982) 'Learning to read culturally: literacy before schooling', in H. Goelman, A. Oberg and F. Smith, (eds) *Awakening to Literacy* (pp. 3–23). Exeter, NH: Heinemann.

Scollon, R. and Scollon, S. (1981) *Narrative, Literacy, and Face in Interethnic Communication*. Norwood, NJ: Ablex.

Scribner, S. and Cole, M. (1978) 'Literacy without schooling'. *Harvard Educational Review* **48**, 448–461.

Shatz, M., Wellman, H. and Silber, S. (1983) 'The acquisition of mental verbs: a systematic investigation of the first reference to mental state'. *Cognition* **14**, 301–331.

Shockley, B., Michalove, B. and Allen, J. (1995) *Engaging Families*. Portsmouth, NH: Heinemann.

Sigel, I. E. and McGillicuddy-DeLisi, A. (1984) 'Parents as teachers of their children: a distancing behavior model', in A. D. Pellegrini and T. D. Yawkey (eds) *The Development of Oral and Written Language in Social Context* (pp. 71–92). Norwood, NJ: Ablex.

Slomkowski, C. (1991) 'Temperament and language'. Paper presented at the biennial meeting of the Society for Research in Child Development, Seattle.

Slomkowski, C. and Dunn, J. (1993) 'Conflict in close relationships'. Paper presented at the biennial meeting of the Society for Research in Child Development, New Orleans.

Smilansky, S. (1967) *The Effect of Social Dramatic Play on Disadvantaged Preschool Children*. New York: Wiley.

Smith, P. K. (1982) 'Does play matter? Functional and evolutionary aspects of animal and human play'. *Behavioral and Brain Sciences* **5**, 139–184.

Smith, P. K. (1988) 'Children's play and its role in early development: a re-evaluation of the '"play ethos"', in A. D. Pellegrini (ed.) *Psychological Bases for Early Education* (pp. 207–226). Chichester: Wiley.

Smith, P. K. and Dodsworth, C. (1978) 'Social class differences in the fantasy play of preschool children'. *Journal of Genetic Psychology* **133**, 183–190.

Smith, P. K. and Hagan, T. (1980) 'Effects of play deprivation on exercise play in nursery school children'. *Animal Behaviour* **28**, 922–928.

Smith, P. K. and Vollstedt, R. (1985) 'On defining play'. *Child Development* **56**, 1042–1050.

Smith, P. K. Takhvar, M., Gore, N. and Vollstedt, R. (1986) 'Play in young children: problems in definition, categorization and measurement', in P. K. Smith (ed.) *Children's Play* (pp. 37–54). London: Gordon and Breach.

Snow, C. (1972) 'Mothers' speech to children learning language'. *Child Development* **43**, 549–565.

Snow, C. (1983) 'Literacy and language: relationships during the preschool years'. *Harvard Educational Review* **53**, 165–189.

Stahl, S. and Murray, B. (1993) 'Defining phonological awareness and its relation to early reading'. Paper presented at the annual meeting of the American Educational Research Association, Atlanta.

Stanovich, K. (1993) 'Does reading make you smarter? Literacy and the development of verbal intelligence', in H. W. Reese (ed.) *Advances in Child Development and Behavior*, vol. 24 (pp. 133–180). New York: Academic Press.

Steinberg L., Dornbusch, S. M. and Brown, B. B. (1992) 'Ethnic differences in adolescent achievement'. *American Psychologist* **47**, 723–729.

Stevenson, H. and Lee, S. (1990) *Contexts of Achievement*. Monographs for the Society for Research in Child Development (serial 221) 55 (1–2).

Sullivan, H. S. (1953) *The Interpersonal Theory of Psychiatry*. New York: Norton.

Sulzby, E. (1987) 'Writing and reading', in E. Sulzby and W. Teale (eds) *Emergent Literacy* (pp. 50–89). Norwood, NJ: Ablex.

Sulzby, E. and Teale, W. (eds) (1987) *Emergent Literacy, Final Report to the Spencer Foundation*. Norwood, NJ: Ablex.

Symons, D. (1978) *Play and Aggression: A Study of Rhesus Monkeys*. New York: Columbia University Press.

Teale, W. (1984) 'Reading to young children: its significance for literacy development', in H. Goelman, A. Oberg and F. Smith (eds) *Awakening to Literacy* (pp. 110–121). Exeter, NH: Heinemann.

Terrill, R. (1973) *R. H. Tawney and His Times*. Cambridge, MA: Harvard University Press.

Tesser. A., Campbell, J. and Smith, M. (1984) 'Friendships choice and performance: self-evaluation maintenance in children'. *Journal of Social and Personality Psychology* **46**, 561–574.

Tinbergen, N. (1963) 'On the aims and methods of ethology'. *Zeitschrift für Tierpsychologie* **20**, 410–433.

Tizard, B. and Hughes, M. (1984) *Young Children Learning*. Cambridge, MA: Harvard University Press.

Tooby, J. and Cosmides, L. (1992) 'The psychological foundations of culture', in J. Barkow, L. Cosmides, and J. Tooby (eds) *The Adapted Mind: Evolutionary Psychology and the Generation of Culture* (pp. 19–136). Oxford: Oxford University Press.

Torrance, N. and Olson, D. R. (1984) 'Oral language competence and the acquisition of literacy', in A. D. Pellegrini and T. D. Yawkey (eds) *The*

Development of Oral and Written Language in Social Context (pp. 167–182). Norwood, NJ: Ablex.

Vachek, J. (1964) *A Prague School Reader*. Bloomington, IN: Indiana University Press.

Vygotsky, L. S. (1962) *Thought and Language*. Cambridge, MA: MIT Press.

Vygotsky, L. S. (1978) *Mind in Society*. Cambridge, MA: Harvard University Press.

Waldrop, M. and Halverson, C. (1975) 'Intensive and extensive peer groups'. *Child Development* **46**, 19–26.

Waters, E. and Sroufe, L. A. (1983) 'Social competence as a developmental construct'. *Developmental Review* **3**, 79–97.

Wechsler, D. (1974) *Manual for the Wechsler Intelligence Scale for Children*. New York: Psychological Corporation.

Wells, G. (1984) *Learning through Interaction*. New York: Cambridge University Press.

Werner, H. and Kaplan, B. (1952) *The Acquisition of Word Meaning*. Monographs for the Society for Research in Child Development (serial 51) 18 (1).

Wertsch, J. V. (1979) 'From social interaction to higher psychological processes'. *Human Development* **22**, 1–22.

Wertsch, J. V., McNamee, G., McLane, D. and Budwig, N. (1980) 'The adult–child dyad as a problem solving system'. *Child Development* **51**, 1215–1221.

Whitehurst, G., Falco, F., Lonigan, J., Fishcel, B., DeBaryshe, B., Valdezmenchaid, B. and Caulfield, M. (1988) 'Accelerating language development through picture book reading'. *Developmental Psychology* **24**, 552–559.

Wolf, D. and Grollman, S. (1982) 'Ways of playing', in D. Pepler and K. Rubin (eds) *The Play of Children* (pp. 46–63). Basel: Karger.

Wolf, D., Davidson, L., Davis, M., Walters, J., Hodges, M. and Scripp, L. (1988) *Psychological Bases of Early Education* (pp. 121–151). Chichester: Wiley.

Index